5th Workshop on Semantic Deep Learning 2019 (SemDeep-5)

Macau, China
12 August 2019

ISBN: 978-1-5108-9142-5

Printed from e-media with permission by:

Curran Associates, Inc.
57 Morehouse Lane
Red Hook, NY 12571

Some format issues inherent in the e-media version may also appear in this print version.

Printed by Curran Associates, Inc. (2019)

For permission requests, please contact the Association for Computational Linguistics at the address below.

Association for Computational Linguistics
209 N. Eighth Street
Stroudsburg, Pennsylvania 18360

Phone: 1-570-476-8006
Fax: 1-570-476-0860

acl@aclweb.org

Additional copies of this publication are available from:

Curran Associates, Inc.
57 Morehouse Lane
Red Hook, NY 12571 USA
Phone: 845-758-0400
Fax: 845-758-2633
Email: curran@proceedings.com
Web: www.proceedings.com

IJCAI 2019

Proceedings of the 5th Workshop on Semantic Deep Learning (SemDeep-5)

12 August, 2019
Macau, China

Preface

Welcome to the 5th Workshop on **Semantic Deep Learning (SemDeep-5)**, held in conjunction with IJ-CAI 2019 (Macau, China). As a series of workshops and a special issue, SemDeep has been aiming to bring together Semantic Web and Deep Learning research as well as industrial communities. It seeks to offer a platform for joining computational linguistics and formal approaches to represent information and knowledge, and thereby opens the discussion for new and innovative application scenarios for neural and symbolic approaches to NLP, such as neural-symbolic reasoning.

SemDeep-5 features a shared task on evaluating meaning representations, the Word in Context (WiC) challenge. It represents a joint task of semantic structure in the organization of senses and their representation. In addition to providing a reliable benchmark for studying an important linguistic phenomenon, WiC is directly related to applications such as word sense disambiguation, entity linking, and semantic search. In brief, the task consists in determining whether a given word is used in the same or different senses given two different contexts. For the WiC challenge there were seven participant systems and three papers could be accepted. Ansell et al. present an ELMo-inspired approach to tackle this challenge that introduces a new similarity measure for an adapted version of contextualized representations. Loureiro and Jorge combine word sense disambiguation with contextual embeddings and sense embeddings. Finally, Soler et al. utilize word and sentence embeddings paired with in-context substitute annotations.

In total, six research papers could be accepted for the workshop, four of which are long papers and two are short, covering a wide variety of topics from neural question answering to knowledge representation and sequential tagging. Hommel et al. evaluate the impact of integrating linguistic features, such as Part-of-Speech (PoS) and syntactic dependency relations, in a state-of-the-art question-answering architecture and find a highly positive effect of this integration. Also along the lines of PoS, Wang et al. analyze cross-linguistic aspects of tagging social media texts and propose a language-agnostic model that utilizes a tagging scheme specific to this text genre, tested in Chinese. Concatenating rich features from a gazetteer with input embeddings also proved as a successful integration strategy in Magnolini et al., who analyze English and Italian data. More towards knowledge representation, Agibetov et al. focus on link prediction utilizing hyperbolic embeddings specifically in the biological domain and Zhou et al. learn household task knowledge from WikiHow descriptions. Finally, Deshmukh et al. extract structured data from unstructured text by treating the problem as a sequence tagging task.

We would like to thank the Program Committee members for their support of this event in form of reviewing and feedback, without whom we would not be able to ensure the overall quality of the workshop.

Organisers:

Dagmar Gromann, Technical University Dresden (TU Dresden), Dresden, Germany
Luis Espinosa-Anke, Cardiff University, Cardiff, United Kingdom
Thierry Declerck, German Research Centre for Artificial Intelligence (DFKI GmbH), Saarbrücken, Germany
Jose Camacho-Collados, Cardiff University, Cardiff, United Kingdom
Mohammad Taher Pilehvar, Iran University of Science and Technology, Iran

Program Committee:

- Marianna Apidianaki, LIMSI-CNRS, Orsay Cedex, France
- Miguel Ballesteros, IBM T.J. Watson Research Center, Yorktown Heights, NY, USA
- Michael Cochez, RWTH University Aachen, Germany
- Christos Christodoulopoulos, Amazon Research Cambridge, UK
- Agata Filipowska, Poznan University of Economics and Business, Poland
- Dario Garcia-Casulla, Barcelona Supercomputing Center (BSC), Barcelona, Spain
- Jorge Gracia Del Río, Ontology Engineering Group, UPM, Spain
- Víctor Gutiérrez Basulto, Cardiff University, Cardiff, UK
- Wei Hu, Nanjing University, China
- Stratos Kontopoulos, Multimedia Knowledge & Social Media Analytics Laboratory, Thessanloniki, Greece
- Brigitte Krenn, Austrian Research Institute for AI, Vienna, Austria
- John McCrae, Insight Centre for Data Analytics, Galway, Ireland
- José Moreno, Universite Paul Sabatier, IRIT, Toulouse, France
- Luis Nieto Piña, University of Goteborg, Goteburg, Sweden
- Sergio Oramas, Universitat Pompeu Fabra, Barcelona, Spain
- Carla Perez Almendros, Cardiff University, Cardiff, UK
- Alessandro Raganato, University of Helsinki, Helsinki, Finnland
- Simon Razniewski, Max-Planck-Institute, Germany
- Martin Riedl, Stuttgart University, Germany
- Francois Scharffe, Columbia University, New York, USA
- Michael Spranger, Sony Computer Science Laboratories Inc., Tokyo, Japan
- Steven Schockaert, Cardiff University, United Kingdom
- Arkaitz Zubiaga, University of Warwick, United Kingdom

Table of Contents

Papers

WiC Papers

Bridging the Gap: Improve Part-of-speech Tagging for Chinese Social Media Texts with Foreign Words

Dingmin Wang[1], **Meng Fang**[2], **Yan Song**[2], **Juntao Li**[3]
[1] Tencent Cloud AI, Shenzhen, Guangdong, China
[2] Tencent AI Lab, Shenzhen, Guangdong, China
[3] Peking University, Beijing, China
{wangdimmy, moefang, mattsure}@gmail.com lijuntao@pku.edu.cn

Abstract

Multilingual speakers often switch between languages and generate enormous quantities of cross-language data. This phenomenon is more frequent observed in social media texts, where a large body of user generated data is produced every day. Such mix-lingual and informal texts lead to a challenge for part-of-speech (POS) tagging, which is one fundamental task in natural language processing. In this paper, we propose a language-agnostic POS tagger for social media texts, which is able to learn from heterogeneous data with different genre and language type. Particularly, in order to comprehensively evaluate POS tagging performance, we propose a new tagging scheme including exclusive tags for special symbols in social media texts, and a human-annotated dataset of Chinese-English mixed social media texts is also developed. Experiments on both synthetic and real datasets show the validity and effectiveness of our model on social media texts where it outperforms state-of-the-art language-specific taggers.

1 Introduction

Part-of-speech tagging is the basic step of identifying a token's functional role within a sentence and is the fundamental step in many NLP pipeline applications. It is well known that the performance of complex NLP systems is negatively affected if one of the preliminary stages is less than perfect. For example, some tagging errors may change the semantic interpretation of an entire sentence, typically due to assigning an entirely incorrect POS category to a word, for example a Plural Noun (NNS) incorrectly tagged as a Present Tense Verb (VBZ). This alteration in the semantics has a deleterious effect on all the subsequent steps in the NLP pipeline, e.g., Syntactic Parsing, Dependency Parsing, etc. Compared with formal texts, like newswire articles, the POS tagging performance in the social media texts is still far from satisfactory (Ritter et al., 2011; Gimpel et al., 2011). Most state-of-the-art POS tagging approaches are based on supervised methods, in which a large amount of annotated data is needed to train models. However, many datasets constructed for the POS tagging task are from carefully-edited newswire articles, such as PTB (Marcus et al., 1993) and CTB (Xia, 2000), which are greatly different from social media texts. The difference in domains between training data and testing data may heavily impact the performance of approaches based on supervised methods. Hence, most state-of-the-art POS taggers cannot achieve the same performance as reported on newswire domain when applied on social media texts (Owoputi et al., 2013).

However, enormous quantities of user generated content on social media are giving increasing attention as well as valuable sources for a variety of applications, such as recommendation (Jiang and Yang, 2017), disease prediction (Paul and Dredze, 2011). Yet, in such NLP tasks, one challenge is that texts from social media platforms (e.g., Twitter[1], Weibo[2]) usually contain many informal inputs, such as acronym (as soon as possible $\rightarrow$ asap), shorthand (technology $\rightarrow$ tech), out-of-vocabulary words (meeeeee $\rightarrow$ me), etc.

Another challenge is that many mix-lingual cases exist in microblogs, which occurs frequently in such informal texts. For example, according to (Zhang et al., 2014), in Weibo[7], the mixed usage of Chinese and English is one of the most popular phenomena with informal language. To illustrate

[1]http://www.twitter.com
[2]http://www.weibo.com
[3]http://nlp.stanford.edu:8080/parser/index.jsp
[4]https://github.com/fxsjy/jieba
[5]http://ictclas.nlpir.org/nlpir/
[6]Since the three POS taggers use different tag sets, so the tags are a little different.
[7]The largest Chinese social media platform.

Sent	今天帮我book一个会议室 help me book a meeting roomt today
Gold	今天/NT 帮我/AD 预定/VV 一/CD 个/M 会议室/NN
ST[3]	今天/NT 帮我/VV book一/CD 个/M 会议室/NN
Jieba[4]	今天/t 帮/v 我/r book/eng 一个/m 会议室/n
NLPIR[5]	今天/T 帮/V 我/RR book/N 一个/MQ 会议室/N

Table 1: Tagging results on an example Chinese-English Weibo by different Chinese POS taggers. Incorrect results are marked in red.[6]

such phenomenon, one example of microblogs extracted from real Weibo texts is shown in Table 1, all of which are written in Chinese with a few English words.

In this paper, we focus on the task of annotating Chinese-English social media texts from Weibo, and implement automatic part-of-speech (POS) tagging of these texts. To this end, we propose an approach to learning a POS tagger that can be applied in truly cross-language social media texts. We discuss techniques that allow us to learn a tagger given only the amount of labeled data that contains standard monolingual languages, specifically. Here, we improve the tagging performance on Weibo texts, which involves Chinese and English, by using the semantic information from different sources of labeled data. Experimental results on both synthetic and real Weibo texts confirm the effectiveness of our method. Our contributions can be concluded as follows:

- We explore to utilize multiple sources of annotated corpora to improve performance on tagging cross-lingual Weibo texts. To this end, we extends the bi-directional long short term network with adversarial training.
- For the first time, we develop a cross-lingual microblog corpus and give a quantitative evaluation for POS tagging in such microblog corpus.
- Experimental results show that our model is better than existing state-of-the-art language specific taggers.

2 Related Work

In essence, this paper is concerned with the intersection of three topics: part-of-speech tagging, processing of social media texts, and language-switching in social media texts:

Part-of-speech tagging is widely treated as a sequence labeling problem, by assigning a unique label over each sentential word (Fang and Cohn, 2016). Early studies on sequence labeling often use the models of HMM (Kupiec, 1992) and CRF (Lafferty et al., 2001) based on manually-crafted discrete features, which can suffer the feature sparsity problem and require heavy feature engineering. Recently, neural network models have been successfully applied to sequence labeling (Collobert and Weston, 2008). Among these work, the model which uses BiLSTM for feature extraction has achieved state-of-the-art performances (Huang et al., 2015), which is exploited as the baseline model in our work.

However, regarding part-of-speech tagging social media texts, the aforementioned methods are seldom used because of limited labeled data. Two most similar earlier papers are the ARK tagger (Gimpel et al., 2011) and T-Pos (Ritter et al., 2011). Both these approaches adopt clustering to handle linguistic noise, and train from a mixture of hand-annotated tweets and existing POS-labeled data. The ARK tagger reaches 92.8 % accuracy at token level but uses a coarse, customized tagset. T-Pos is based on the Penn Treebank dataset and achieves an 88.4% token tagging accuracy.

In recent years, there have been several efforts on social media text POS tagging, but almost exclusively on Twitter and mostly for English. However, it is noted that there are limited work on POS tagging cross-language texts, especially for Chinese-English texts. (Moschitti et al., 2014) reports achieving an accuracy of over 90% on English-Hindi texts and (Lascarides et al., 2009) propose a method to combine rule-based and statistically induced taggers on handling cross-language texts. However, these work on POS tagging cross-language texts can not be directly used to Chinese-English due to the great difference between languages.

3 The Model

3.1 Overview

For most of Chinese POS taggers, there are usually two kinds of ways to tag foreign words: one is to directly tag them as "foreign words", which is oversimplified; another is to give a POS tag simply based on a rule-based method, which is easy to make incorrect tags and influences the further processing for the syntactic and semantic analysis. To

Type	Input	Segmentation & Part-Of-Speech
Zh-only	我希望你去采用下我的方法	我/PN 希望/VV 你去/AD 采用/VV 下/DT 我/PN 的/DEG 方法/NN
Mixed	我希望你去follow下我的方法	我/PN 希望/VV 你去/VV follow/NN 下/LC 我/PN 的/DEG 方法/NN

Table 2: POS tagging results by Standford POS Tagger [8]. Incorrect results are marked in red.

illustrate the challenge, we take one of the state-of-the-art Chinese POS taggers (Standford Chinese POS tagger) as an example. From Table 2, we can see that when the input only contains Chinese words, the tagger can do a completely correct tagging. But, when we replace a Chinese word "采用" with its corresponding English translation "follow", we find that the tagger gives an incorrect tag "NN" to "follow". A possible reason is that Stanford Chinese POS tagger trains only on the Chinese corpus, so it is "dull" to unseen English words. However, this situation happens a lot in social media, such as Weibo.

Our goal is to train a POS tagger for Chinese social media data, which contains user-generated content and cross-language short text, specifically Chinese-English text. Because there lacks annotated Chinese social media data, we consider making use of out-of-domain (e.g., CTB (Xia, 2000)) and labeled data from other languages (e.g., PTB (Marcus et al., 1993), ARK (Gimpel et al., 2011)), which are carefully annotated and widely used in NLP-related tasks. The basic model is shown in Figure 1, with its inputs from different sources of labeled annotated data and the output being a sequence of POS tags for the given sentence. The feasibility of our method are based on the following three points:

- We use a pre-trained cross-lingual embedding, where words across two languages share same semantic space, so their semantic proximity could be correctly quantified.

- Previous work (Yang et al., 2017) has shown that *knowledge transfer* is an effective method on improving performance on a target task with few labeled training datasets. In our setting, the knowledge learned from Chinese and English datasets can be considered as a process of *knowledge transfer*, which jointly contribute to our task of tagging cross-lingual texts.

- An adversarial network is implemented to improve the share representation, aiming at achieving better tagging performance on cross-lingual texts.

Recent advances suggest that recurrent neural networks are capable of learning useful representation information for modeling problems of sequential nature (Plank et al., 2016). In this section, we describe our social media POS tagger, which is based on bidirectional long short term memory (BiLSTM). Since there is lack of annotated social media data as training data, we consider using other out-of-domain labeled data and labeled from different languages, both of which are monolingual. Instead of the common monolingual embeddings, we use cross-lingual embeddings as a bridge between different languages. Our joint model is trained based on different labeled datasets from different domains and languages. Furthermore, we improve the proposed joint model with an adversarial training scheme.

3.2 Cross-lingual Token Representation

Considering that we need to tag texts containing different languages, i.e. Chinese and English, we hope semantics-close words from different languages can have close distributed word representations. Distributed word representations are useful in NLP applications such as information retrieval, search query expansions, or representing semantics of words. A number of methods have been explored to train and apply word embeddings using continuous models for language-specific corpora. However, Chinese- and English- embeddings trained from their own language-specific corpora usually share a totally different semantic space since each language has its own vocabulary space. Therefore, although the Chinese word "政府" shares the same knowledge semantics with its English translation "government", their distance in the distributed word representation space is not close as we expect. Specially, we adopt two approaches to train a bilingual embeddings.

3.2.1 Unsupervised Training

We adopt the method proposed in (Zou et al., 2013) to achieve bilingual embeddings. First, by

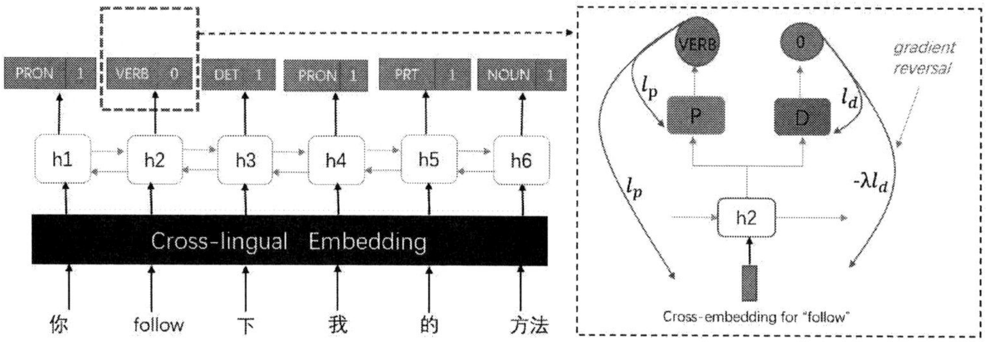

Figure 1: The general architecture of our proposed model. The green box and red box represents two feed-forward networks, which are used for the tagging task and the language identification task, respectively. Note that we only show the operation on the one hidden state of BiLSTM's outputs, and other hidden states have the same operation.

using the machine translation word alignments extracted with the Berkeley Aligner (Liang et al., 2006), two alignment matrices ($A_{zh\rightarrow en}$, $A_{en\rightarrow zh}$) are achieved. Next, two combined objectives are optimized during training:

$$J_{CO-zh} + \lambda J_{TEO-en\rightarrow zh} \quad (1)$$

$$J_{CO-en} + \lambda J_{TEO-zh\rightarrow en} \quad (2)$$

Equation 1 and 2 are optimized for Chinese embeddings and English embeddings, respectively. For example, for Chinese embedding, J_{CO-zh} is to keep the monolingual features of Chinese language itself, and $J_{TEO-en\rightarrow zh}$ is to optimize the Translation Equivalence. The embeddings are learned through curriculum training on the Chinese Gigaword corpus.

3.2.2 Embedding Projection

Instead of training embeddings joint for two languages, we consider using existing embeddings with projection. There are many available pretrained word embeddings trained from monolingual corpora. Considering that in Weibo, most of texts are written in Chinese, we project the English embedding space (S) into the Chinese embedding space (T). Instead of re-training from parallel corpora, we adopt two methods proposed in (Song and Lee, 2017) to do the embedding projection. We get 1,000 common Chinese words and its corresponding English translations, which will be used to calculate the projection function. In linear projection, the least square fitting is used to solve the projection formula. For non-linear projection, the projection is implemented with a two-layer perceptron.

3.3 The Joint Model

To utilize a set of labeled corpora from different domains and languages to improve the tagging performance on cross-lingual Weibo texts, we first consider a joint model based on *knowledge transfer*. To facilitate this, we give an explanation for notations used in this paper. Formally, we refer to S_k as a collection of source training datasets from k labeled corpora. Mathematically,

$$S_k = \{d_i\}_{i=1}^{k} \quad (3)$$

$$d_i = \{(x_j^i, y_j^i)\}_{j=1}^{L_i} \quad (4)$$

$$x_j^i = \{w_m\}_{m=1}^{N} \quad (5)$$

$$y_j^i = \{t_m\}_{m=1}^{N}, t_m \in T, \quad (6)$$

where L_i represents the number of sentences in the corpus d_i; x_j^i and y_j^i denote a sentence and a set of tags for the sentence from d_i, respetively; N is the length of the given sentence, namely, the number of words; w_m and t_m denote a word and its corresponding POS tag, respectively; T is a set of POS tags defined in our paper, which will be described in Section 3.4.

3.3.1 The Part-of-speech Tagging Model

Let $\{x_1, \cdots, x_n\}$ be the sequence of words and $\{y_1, \cdots, y_n\}$be the sequence of POS tags. We define the joint distribution as follows:

$$p(t_1, t_2, \cdots, t_n | x_1, x_2, \cdots, x_n) = \prod_{i=1} n p(y_i | x_1, x_2, \cdots, x_n), \quad (7)$$

where $p(y_i|x_1, x_2, \cdots, x_n)$ uses a bidirectional long short term memory (BiLSTM) (Graves and

Schmidhuber, 2005). The update of each LSTM unit can be written as follows:

$$\overleftarrow{h_t}, \overrightarrow{h_t} = \text{BiLSTM}(h_{t-1}; x_t; \theta), \quad (8)$$

where x_t is a input at the current time step, h_{t-1} is hidden value of last time step, and θ represents all parameters.

For the given sequence $x = (x_1, x_2, \cdots, x_n)$, we first use an embedding layer to get the vector representation (mix-lingual embeddings) of each word x_i. The output at the last moment h_t can be regarded as the representation of the whole sequence, which has a fully connected layer followed by a softmax non-linear layer that predicts the probability distribution over classes.

$$\hat{y} = \text{softmax}(W_p(\overleftarrow{h_t} + \overrightarrow{h_t}) + b_p), \quad (9)$$

where $\hat{y}$ is prediction probabilities, W_p is the weights which need to be learned, b_p is a bias term. Given a corpus with N training samples (x_i, y_i), the parameters of the network are trained to minimise the cross-entropy of the predicted and true distributions.

$$l_p(\hat{y}, y) = -\sum_{i=1}^{N}\sum_{j=1}^{C} y_i^j \log \hat{y}_i^j, \quad (10)$$

where y_i^j is the ground-truth label;$\hat{y}_i^j$ is prediction probabilities, and C is the class number.

3.3.2 Adversarial Training

The network described so far learns the abstract features through hidden layers that are discriminative for the part-of-speech tagging task. However, our goal is also to make these features invariant across languages in order to adapt to cross-lingual texts. To this end, we incorporate the adversarial training into our baseline POS tagger. Adversarial training (Goodfellow et al., 2014) is a powerful regularization method, which have been explored in the domain adaption (Ganin et al., 2016) and image recognition (Shrivastava et al., 2017) to improve the robustness of classifiers to input perturbations. We introduce a language discriminator, another neural network that takes the output hidden state of the BiLSTM network as input at each time step, and tries to discriminate between Chinese and English inputs in our case. Mathematically, the language discriminator is defined by a sigmoid function, and the discrimination loss is represented as the negative log-probability:

$$l_d = d\log(\hat{d}) + (1-d)\log(1-\hat{d}) \quad (11)$$

Special Word	Example	Tag
Text Emoji	:-D	EMOT
Pictorial Emoji	[:-D]	EMOJ
URLs	https://weibo.com	URL
Tel Number	88888	PHONE
At-mention	@邓超	MENT
Topic	#爸爸去哪儿#	Hash

Table 3: Six specific tags for Weibo texts

where $d \in \{0, 1\}$ denotes the language label (1 for Chinese and 0 for English), and $\hat{d}$ is the predicted probability for $d = 1$.

The overall training objective of the joint model can be written as follows:

$$l = l_p - \lambda l_d \quad (12)$$

where the hyper-parameter λ controls the relative strength of the two networks.

Specifically, in our gradient descent training, the optimization is performed by reversing the gradients of the language discrimination loss l_d (Ganin et al., 2016), when they are backpropagated to the shared layers. As shown in Figure 1, the gradient reversal is applied to the BiLSTM layer and also to the layers that come before it.

3.4 Part-of-Speech Tagsets

Since we use labeled datasets from different domains and languages, we need to map different tagsets to a uniform tagset. To do so, we use the 12 universal POS tags defined in (Petrov et al., 2011): NOUN (nouns), VERB (verbs), ADJ (adjectives), ADV (adverbs), PRON (pronouns), DET (determiners and articles), ADP (prepositions and postpositions), NUM (numerals), CONJ (conjunctions), PRT (particles), '.' (punctuation marks) and X (a catch-all for other categories)[9].

Besides, we design additional 6 tags specific to Weibo texts: text emoticons; pictorial emoticons; URLs; telephone number; Weibo hashtags, of the form #tagname#, which the author may supply to categorize a Weibo post; and Weibo at-mentions, of the form @user, which link to other Weibo users from within a Weibo post. The details of 6 social media tags are shown in Table 3.

[9]The mapping rules for different tagsets are obtained from https://github.com/slavpetrov/universal-pos-tags.

Name	# of Sen	# of Chinese	of English	# of Other
S-weibo	1,000	10,901	1221	343
R-weibo	700	6,071	878	223

Table 4: Statistics of synthetic and manually-annotated datasets, denoted as S-weibo and M-weibo, respectively. (# of Chinese, English, Other denotes the number of words, respectively.)

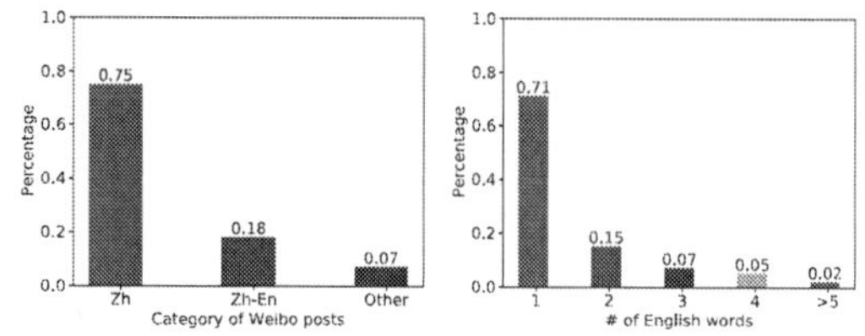

Figure 2: **Left**: Language distribution in Weibo posts. (Zh: only contains Chinese words; Zh-En: contains both Chinese and English words; Other: contains words of more than two different languages); **Right**: English words percentage in the Chinese-English mixed Weibo posts

4 Experiments

This section explains our experiments on the evaluation of our proposed model on POS tagging cross-lingual Weibo texts. First, we describe how we collect and annotate Weibo texts. A synthetic method to generate language mixed Weibo texts is also illustrated. Both of datasets are only used for testing. Next, we explore the utility of cross-lingual embeddings generated by the aforementioned two methods: unsupervised training and embedding projection. Then, we evaluate the proposed model on both the synthetic and manually-annotated datasets.

4.1 Data Collection and Annotation

Synthetic Without annotated language mixed posts from Weibo, we first propose a synthetic method to generate such data as an alternative. Considering that in Chinese-English mixed posts, English words of noun, verb and adjective categories are the most commonly used, so we randomly transform a certain percentage of Chinese words with these POS tags. An annotated Chinese-only Weibo dataset are obtained from NLPCC 2015 Shared Task (Li et al., 2015).

Manual Annotation To validate the actual performance, we develop a corpus by manually annotating text messages posted to Weibo. Initially, we collect $500,000$ raw Weibo posts using Weibo API on December 6, 2017. The posts are on various 'hot' topics (i.e., topics that are currently being discussed in news, social media, etc.). These raw posts are then divided into three categories: Chinese-only, Chinese-English and Other. The language distribution of these posts and the frequency of English words used in the Chinese-English posts shown are shown in Figure 2. We can see that over 70% mix-lingual Weibo posts only contain one English word.

Next, we randomly choose 700 posts containng both Chinese and English. Then, we ask three trained annotators to do the annotation task. Unlike English language, a Chinese word usually consists of two or more characters, so we need to segment the posts before the annotation of the POS tagging. In order to speed up the manual annotation, we first pre-segment the 700 posts using a Chinese Word Segmenter (Jieba), and these segmented posts are then proofread and modified by two trained annotators. Finally, two trained annotators are asked to tag the segmented posts using the 18 POS tags. Lastly, we ask the third annotator to tag those words that are differently tagged by the previous two annotators. Details of our experiment datasets are shown in Table 4.

4.2 Experimental Setup

Our training data mainly consists of three sources: PTB (Marcus et al., 1993), ARK (Gimpel et al., 2011), and CTB (Xia, 2000). Different tagsets are all mapped into the universal tagset described in Section 3.4. Notice that since ARK is collected from Twitter, also a kind of social media data, so we keep Tweet-specific tags and map them to our defined 6 Weibo-specific tags, for the reason that some marks also appear in Weibo texts, such as At-methion, URLs, and so on. We use three language-specific Chinese POS taggers (ST, Jieba, NLPIR) as our baseline models.

Besides, two models with and without adversarial training, denoted as BiLSTM$^-$ and BiLSTM$^+$, are implemented to study the utility of the adversarial training in our task. The hyper-parameters used for our model are as follows:

- **BiLSTM$^-$**: The hidden size is set to 150 and other hyper-parameters are tuned on a development set consisting of 10% randomly selected sentences from the training data. RMSprop (Graves, 2013) is used as optimizer.

Corpus	Models	English Word					Chinese Word	Weibo Word
		OOV	NOUN	VERB	ADJ	Other		
S-weibo	ST	\	0.611	0.802	0.557	\	0.901	0.936
	Jieba	\	0	0	0	\	0.929	0.936
	NLPI	\	0.691	0.866	0.628	\	**0.930**	0.936
	BiLSTM$^-$	\	0.701	0.863	0.708	\	0.908	0.936
	BiLSTM$^+$	\	**0.756**	**0.871**	**0.727**	\	0.912	0.936
R-weibo	ST	0.494	0.594	0.746	0.708	0.582	0.907	0.921
	Jieba	0	0	0	0	0	0.896	0.921
	NLPI	0.492	0.621	0.758	0.781	0.651	**0.918**	0.921
	BiLSTM$^-$	0.628	0.702	0.801	0.652	0.682	0.894	0.921
	BiLSTM$^+$	**0.672**	**0.731**	**0.812**	**0.703**	**0.697**	0.900	0.921

Table 5: Experimental results (F1 scores) on synthetic and manually-annoated testing datasets, denoted as **S-weibo** and **R-weibo**, respectively. In **S-weibo**, we only replace three types of English words using rules, so there is no OOV and other English words in it. Besides, the Chinese POS tagger Jieba tags all foreign words as "eng", so its F1 scores are all considered to be 0 with regard to English words.

Emebdding	Method	Train-Data	Test-data	Accuracy
Uns-emb	BiLSTM	PTB(en)	CTB(zh)	**0.511**
	BiLSTM	CTB(zh)	PTB(en)	**0.486**
Lprj-emb	BiLSTM	PTB(en)	CTB(zh)	0.346
	BiLSTM	CTB(zh)	PTB(en)	0.310
Nprj-emb	BiLSTM	PTB(en)	CTB(zh)	0.467
	BiLSTM	CTB(zh)	PTB(en)	0.406

Table 6: Experimental results by different cross-lingual embeddings (Uns-emb, Lprj-emb, Nprj-emb are cross-embeddings generated by unsupervised training, linear embedding projection and non-linear embedding projection, respectively).

- **BiLSTM$^+$**: We extend BiLSTM with an adversarial training, aiming at improving the share representation. The setting in the part of BiLSTM is same with the baseline BiLSTM. We adjust the discriminative ratio by multiple iterations of adversarial training.

4.3 Exploration of Cross-lingual Embeddings

Chinese and English have many similarities in the utterance, even if they have their own grammar rules. Therefore, with a joint semantic space of words across languages, it is possible that knowledge can be transferred from one language to another, and we can tag a corpus without having training data that has the same language with it. 6 sets of experiments are designed, where the effectiveness of cross-lingual embedding generated by three different methods is evaluated. The criteria is the POS tagging performance and we use BiLSTM as the evaluation model. In Table 6, we use cross-lingual embeddings and train a BiLSTM only on monolingual data. However, we still get a comparative cross-lingual tagging performance. In using the PTB (Marcus et al., 1993), an English annotated newswire corpus, as training data, we get a 51.1% accuracy on tagging CTB, a Chinese corpus (Xia, 2000). By the experiment, we can see that cross-lingual embeddings generated by the unsupervised training method achieve the best tagging performance. Therefore, in the following experiments, if not particularly specified, we use the cross-lingual embeddings trained by the unsupervised method.

4.4 Evaluation Results

Table 5 shows the experimental results on both synthetic and real cross-lingual Weibo posts. In terms of the tagging performance of Chinese words, our model achieves a comparable tagging performance when compared with the other three Chinese POS taggers (0.912 and 0.900, which are 0.19 and 0.18 less than the best results, respectively). One possible reason is that since our model utilizes training datasets from different languages and domains, the tag selection may be impacted by multiple factors and compromised when compared with models trained on the training data containing only one language .

However, our model achieves the best results on tagging different types of English words, which shows the effectiveness of our model. In addition, from the tagging result of Weibo words, we can see that using template rules can achieve a good performance, 0.936 and 0.921 in **S-weibo** and **R-weibo**, respectively. In Weibo (or other social

metric	sentence-level	word-level
F1-score	**0.68**	0.61

Table 7: Comparison of POS tagging performance on English words of **R-weibo** by using sentence-level and word-level translation approaches.

media texts), these social symbols are rather limited and can be easily detected, and using template rules is enough to achieve a satisfactory result.

4.5 Exploration of Translation Function

For a sentence containing both Chinese and English words, we explore the POS tagging performance by utilizing the translation system[10] and the language-specific POS tagger[11]. The language-mixed sentence is translated and then we use the language-specific POS tagger to do the tagging. In particular, we adopt two methods to do the translation as follows:

Sentence-level Translation The whole sentence is input to the translation system, and the translated results of English words may be affected by other Chinese words.

Word-level Translation In this setting, without providing the context words , we translate the English words one by one and select the first result output by the translation system if there are multiple translation results.

The experimental results on **R-weibo** are shown in Table 7. We can observe that the sentence-level translation gives the better performance. A possible reason is that with a context, the translation system can give a better translation prediction when an English word corresponds to many Chinese expressions. However, such method is oversimplified and the performance is lower than that of our proposed method shown in Table 5, which further validates the utility of our model.

Case Analysis Two real Chinese-English Weibo posts are tagged using Standford Tagger and our model, and the tagged results are shown in Table 8. In the first case, the "push" is a verb in English but is used as an adjective in the current Chinese-English text. The Standford tagger gives an incorrect tag "VERB" for "push" while our model gives the correct tagging result, which

Sent	这个老师太push∗ >︵< ∗ Translation: This teacher is too strict ∗ >︵< ∗
ST	这个/DET 老师/NOUN 太/ADV push/VERB ∗ >︵< ∗/EMOJ
BiLSTM$^+$	这个/DET 老师/NOUN 太/ADV push/ADJ ∗ >︵< ∗/EMOJ
Sent	整个场面我要Hold住 Transalation: I need to hold the whole scene
ST	整个/DET 场面/NOUN 我/PRON 要/VERB Hold/ADV 住/VERB
BiLSTM$^+$	整个/DET 场面/NOUN 我/PRON 要/VERB Hold/VERB 住/VERB

Table 8: Comparison results on two real cross-lingual Weibo posts by Standford tagger and our model, respectively. Incorrect results are marked in red.[12]

shows that our model have learned the knowledge at both syntactic and semantic level via both Chinese and English source data. Likewise, the English word "Hold" in the second case should serve as a verb as most of cases in English, but Standford tagger gives a completely incorrect tag, which indicates the constraints of language-specific taggers in handling cross-lingual texts while shows the robustness and utility of our model.

5 Conclusion

Language mixing has become a popular social phenomenon, especially in informal text such as Weibo and Twitter. In this paper, we focus on POS tagging on Chinese social media texts via learning from multiple sources of labeled corpora. To improve tagging performance on social media texts, adversarial training is adopted in our model to reduce the bias of the tagger on different languages. Experimental results confirm the validity of our approach. Compared with existing state-of-the-art language-specific taggers, our model achieves a better performance on tagging cross-lingual social media texts. We believe that our results provide a strong baseline in part-of-speech tagging Chinese social media texts.

References

Ronan Collobert and Jason Weston. 2008. A Unified Architecture for Natural Language Processing: Deep Neural Networks with Multitask Learning. In *Proceedings of the 25th international conference on Machine learning*, pages 160–167. ACM.

Meng Fang and Trevor Cohn. 2016. Learning When to Trust Distant Supervision: An Application to Low-resource POS Tagging Using Cross-lingual Projection. *arXiv preprint arXiv:1607.01133*.

[10] http://fanyi.baidu.com

[11] Chinese POS tagger.http://ictclas.nlpir.org/nlpir/

[12] All tags are mapped to the twelve universal tags plus six our customized social tags as described before.

Yaroslav Ganin, Evgeniya Ustinova, Hana Ajakan, Pascal Germain, Hugo Larochelle, François Laviolette, Mario Marchand, and Victor Lempitsky. 2016. Domain-adversarial Training of Neural Networks. *JMLR*, 17(1):2096–2030.

Kevin Gimpel, Nathan Schneider, Brendan O'Connor, Dipanjan Das, Daniel Mills, Jacob Eisenstein, Michael Heilman, Dani Yogatama, Jeffrey Flanigan, and Noah A Smith. 2011. Part-of-speech Tagging for Twitter: Annotation, Features, and Experiments. In *ACL:short papers-Volume 2*, pages 42–47. Association for Computational Linguistics.

Ian J. Goodfellow, Jonathon Shlens, and Christian Szegedy. 2014. Explaining and harnessing adversarial examples. *CoRR*, abs/1412.6572.

Alex Graves. 2013. Generating Sequences With Recurrent Neural Networks. *arXiv pre-print*, abs/1308.0850.

Alex Graves and Jürgen Schmidhuber. 2005. Framewise phoneme classification with bidirectional LSTM and other neural network architectures. *Neural Networks*, 18(5-6):602–610.

Zhiheng Huang, Wei Xu, and Kai Yu. 2015. Bidirectional LSTM-CRF Models for Sequence Tagging. *arXiv preprint arXiv:1508.01991*.

Ling Jiang and Christopher C. Yang. 2017. User recommendation in healthcare social media by assessing user similarity in heterogeneous network. *Artificial Intelligence in Medicine*, 81:63–77.

Julian Kupiec. 1992. Robust Part-of-speech Tagging using a Hidden Markov Model. *Computer Speech & Language*, 6(3):225–242.

John Lafferty, Andrew McCallum, and Fernando CN Pereira. 2001. Conditional Random Fields: Probabilistic Models for Segmenting and Labeling Sequence Data.

Alex Lascarides, Claire Gardent, and Joakim Nivre, editors. 2009. *EACL, Proceedings of the Conference, Athens, Greece, March 30 - April 3, 2009*. The Association for Computer Linguistics.

Juanzi Li, Heng Ji, Dongyan Zhao, and Yansong Feng, editors. 2015. *Natural Language Processing and Chinese Computing - 4th CCF Conference, Nanchang, China, October 9-13, 2015, Proceedings*, volume 9362 of *Lecture Notes in Computer Science*. Springer.

Percy Liang, Ben Taskar, and Dan Klein. 2006. Alignment by Agreement. In *NAACL*, pages 104–111. Association for Computational Linguistics.

Mitchell P Marcus, Mary Ann Marcinkiewicz, and Beatrice Santorini. 1993. Building a large annotated corpus of english: The penn treebank. *Computational linguistics*, 19(2):313–330.

Alessandro Moschitti, Bo Pang, and Walter Daelemans, editors. 2014. *EMNLP, October 25-29, 2014, Doha, Qatar, A meeting of SIGDAT, a Special Interest Group of the ACL*. ACL.

Olutobi Owoputi, Brendan O'Connor, Chris Dyer, Kevin Gimpel, Nathan Schneider, and Noah A. Smith. 2013. Improved part-of-speech tagging for online conversational text with word clusters. In *NAACL-HLT, June, 9-14, 2013, Atlanta, Georgia, USA*, pages 380–390.

Michael J. Paul and Mark Dredze. 2011. You are what you tweet: Analyzing twitter for public health. In *Proceedings of the Fifth International Conference on Weblogs and Social Media, Barcelona, Catalonia, Spain, July 17-21, 2011*.

Slav Petrov, Dipanjan Das, and Ryan McDonald. 2011. A Universal Part-of-speech Tagset. *arXiv preprint arXiv:1104.2086*.

Barbara Plank, Anders Søgaard, and Yoav Goldberg. 2016. Multilingual part-of-speech tagging with bidirectional long short-term memory models and auxiliary loss. In *ACL, August 7-12, 2016, Berlin, Germany, Volume 2: Short Papers*.

Alan Ritter, Sam Clark, Oren Etzioni, et al. 2011. Named Entity Recognition in Tweets: An Experimental Study. In *EMNLP*, pages 1524–1534. Association for Computational Linguistics.

Ashish Shrivastava, Tomas Pfister, Oncel Tuzel, Joshua Susskind, Wenda Wang, and Russell Webb. 2017. Learning from simulated and unsupervised images through adversarial training. In *CVPR, Honolulu, HI, USA, July 21-26, 2017*, pages 2242–2251.

Yan Song and Chia-Jung Lee. 2017. Embedding projection for query understanding. In *WWW, Perth, Australia, April 3-7, 2017*, pages 839–840.

Fei Xia. 2000. The part-of-speech tagging guidelines for the penn chinese treebank (3.0). *IRCS Technical Reports Series*, page 38.

Zhilin Yang, Ruslan Salakhutdinov, and William W. Cohen. 2017. Transfer learning for sequence tagging with hierarchical recurrent networks. *CoRR*, abs/1703.06345.

Qi Zhang, Huan Chen, and Xuanjing Huang. 2014. Chinese-English Mixed Text Normalization. In *Proceedings of the 7th ACM international conference on Web search and data mining*, pages 433–442. ACM.

Will Y Zou, Richard Socher, Daniel Cer, and Christopher D Manning. 2013. Bilingual Word Embeddings for Phrase-based Machine Translation. In *Proceedings of the 2013 Conference on Empirical Methods in Natural Language Processing*, pages 1393–1398.

Using hyperbolic large-margin classifiers for biological link prediction

Asan Agibetov[1,*] **Georg Dorffner**[1] **Matthias Samwald**[1]
[1]Section for Artificial Intelligence and Decision Support, Medical University of Vienna, Austria
*asan.agibetov@meduniwien.ac.at

Abstract

Recently proposed hyperbolic neural embeddings naturally represent latent hierarchical semantic relations, and could provide a suitable bridge from the discrete world of biological networks to continuous geometric representations, enabling down-stream machine learning tasks, such as link prediction. In some cases, however, link prediction is modeled by separating hyperbolic embeddings using classifiers that operate in a flat Euclidean space, thus underexploiting the inherently curved geometric space of embeddings. Herein we present and analyze how recently introduced large-margin classifiers in hyperbolic space could be used in conjunction with hyperbolic embeddings, in order to perform biological link prediction, which exploits the curved geometry of complex biological information.

1 Introduction

Link prediction is the task of finding missing or unknown links among inter-connected entities. This assumes that entities and links can be represented as a graph, where entities are nodes and links are edges (if relationships are symmetric) or arcs (if relationships are asymmetric). When dealing with link prediction in knowledge bases, the semantic information contained is usually encoded as a knowledge graph (KG) (Sri Nurdiati and Hoede, 2008). For the purposes of this work we simply treat a knowledge graph as a graph with labelled edges (arcs), meaning that two entities may be connected with more than one link of different types. In addition, we conform to the *closed-world* assumption. This means that all the existing (asserted) links are considered *positive*, and all the links which are unknown are considered *negative*. This separation into positive and negative links naturally allows us to treat the link prediction problem as a supervised classification problem with binary classifiers (one classifier for each relation type). However, while this separation makes it possible to use a wide array of well-studied machine learning algorithms for link prediction, the main challenge is how to find the best representations for the links. This is the core subject of the recent research trend in learning suitable representations for knowledge graphs, largely dominated by so-called *neural embeddings*. Most commonly, neural embeddings are numeric representations of nodes and relations of the knowledge graph in some continuous space with vectorial structure. An overview of state-of-the-art approaches can be found in (Nickel et al., 2016).

Predicting links is especially relevant in the biomedical domain, where biological knowledge lends itself naturally to be modelled with knowledge graphs. Indeed, biological entities such as genes and gene functions can be modelled as nodes, and links among these entities as edges or arcs. Neural embeddings Θ for these biological entities could be trained with embedding models. And by training a binary classifier on these continuous numeric representations Θ, we could, for example, estimate the probability $P_l((u, v) = 1 \mid \Theta)$ of having a link l = HAS-FUNCTION (e.g., labelled edge) between nodes u = TRIM28 GENE and v = NEGATIVE REGULATION OF TRANSCRIPTION BY RNA POLYMERASE II.

More recently, researchers in machine learning have turned their attention to hyperbolic space as a better candidate for continuous geometric representation of graph-based data (Nickel and Kiela, 2017; Chamberlain et al., 2017; De Sa et al., 2018; Nickel and Kiela, 2018). This approach could be of special interest for the representation of complex biological networks, which were found to inherently exhibit a hyperbolic structure (Krioukov et al., 2010; Alanis-Lobato et al., 2016). However, as argued in (Cho et al., 2018), in many situations hyperbolic embeddings are used in classification tasks (such as link prediction) that operate in ill-fitted Euclidean space. This leads to a situation where (flat) Euclidean classifiers misuse all the learned curved information that lives in hyperbolic embeddings.

Contribution of this work. In this work we compare hyperbolic and Euclidean large-margin classifiers when used for biological link prediction with the embeddings learned in flat and curved geometric spaces. We believe that the lessons learned from this comparison will help in the identification of next steps required for end-to-end hyperbolic embedding training pipelines to adequately exploit inherently curved geometry, and to uncover latent hierarchical semantic relations of complex biological patterns.

2 Background and Methods

Hyperbolic space can not be embedded without distortion in Euclidean space (Efimov, 1963), however, there are several useful models of hyperbolic geometry formulated as a subset of Euclidean space. Two related models of hyperbolic space, popular in the deep learning community, are *hyperboloid* and *Poincare-ball*. In the first model of n-dimensional hyperbolic geometry points are represented on the forward sheet of a two-sheeted hyperboloid (generalization of hyperbola) of $(n+1)$-dimensional Minkowski space. Minkowski space, roughly speaking, is a linear ambient space endowed with a bilinear metric (generalization of inner product) given by $\langle u, v\rangle_{n+1} = -u_0 v_0 + \sum_{i=1}^{n} u_i v_i$. Thus, an n-dimensional hyperboloid $\mathbb{H}^n$ is a collection of points $\mathbb{H}^n = \{x \in \mathbb{R}^{n+1} | \langle x, x\rangle_{n+1} = 1, x_{n+1} > 0\}$. Under this setting, the distance between two points on the hyperboloid is computed with $d_{\mathbb{H}^n}(u, v) = \cosh^{-1}(-\langle u, v\rangle_{n+1})$. The second model of hyperbolic space is obtained by projecting each point of $\mathbb{H}^n$ onto the hyperplane $x_0 = 0$ using the rays emanating from $(-1, 0, \ldots, 0)$. The latter gives us a *Poincare ball model*, identified with the collection of points $\mathbb{B}^n = \{x : (x_0, \ldots, x_n) \in \mathbb{R}^n \mid \|x\|^2 < 1\}$.

Both models have found their use in literature. On one hand, the Poincare ball model is more intuitive to visualize in lower dimensions (Nickel and Kiela, 2017). On the other hand, a hyperboloid model permits much simpler expression for parameter updates with Riemannian gradient descent, and makes computation significantly faster (Wilson and Leimeister, 2018; Nickel and Kiela, 2018). These two models are equivalent and points can be converted via diffeomorphisms from one space to another. Hyperboloid to Poincare ball with $p(x_0, \ldots, x_n) = \frac{(x_1, \ldots, x_n)}{x_0+1}$, and reciprocally with its inverse $p^{-1}(x_1, \ldots, x_n) = \frac{(1+\|x\|^2, 2x_1, \ldots, 2x_n)}{1-\|x\|^2}$.

Datasets. In this work we consider two biological knowledge graphs: UMLS (subset of the Unified Medical Language System (Bodenreider, 2004) semantic network) and BIO-KG (Alshahrani et al., 2017). BIO-KG is a comprehensive and curated biological knowledge graph that incorporates knowledge from several biological ontologies and databases, including human protein interactions, human chemical-protein interactions and drug side effects and drug indication pairs. UMLS has 46 relation types, 137 biological entities and a total number of 6257 links, BIO-KG has 9 relation types, 346,225 biological entities and 1,619,239 links in total.

Neural embedding models. We compare two shallow semi-supervised neural embedding models (Nickel and Kiela, 2017; Agibetov and Samwald, 2018), which aim at learning *entity embeddings* Θ in a d-dimensional Hyperbolic $\mathbb{H}^d$ and Euclidean $\mathbb{R}^d$ spaces, respectively. Both models are simple. They embed observed connected pairs of entities (positives) close to each other, and place entities that do not share any links (generated negatives) farther apart. As in many neural embedding approaches, the weight matrix Θ of the hidden layer of the neural network represents entity embeddings (latent representations). The neural network is trained by minimizing, for each observed connected pair (u, v), the following loss function

$$\arg\min_{\Theta} \mathcal{L}(\Theta) := \sum_{(u,v)} \log \frac{e^{-d(\Theta(u),\Theta(v))}}{\sum_{(u,v')\in Neg_u} e^{-d(\Theta(u),\Theta v')}}, \quad (1)$$

where $\Theta(u)$ is the currently learned d-dimensional representation of entity u, and Neg_u represents all negative pairs of u (i.e., u, v' do not share any link). Both models have the same signature, but operate in different spaces, which means that distance d and parameters Θ are computed/updated differently. For the hyperbolic model we employ the hyperbolic distance $d_{\mathbb{H}^n}$ and Riemanian SGD with geodesic updates (Wilson and Leimeister, 2018), the implementation of which is available on GitHub [1]. The Euclidean model is trained with StarSpace toolkit [2]; details on preparing data and training neural embeddings with this model can be found in (Agibetov and Samwald, 2018).

Large-margin classification in Hyperbolic space. In (Cho et al., 2018) authors propose Hyperbolic Linear Support Vector classification as the extension of the well-known Euclidean SVM to hyperbolic geometry. Analogously to the Euclidean case, we consider a set of decision functions that lead to linear decision boundaries in the hyperbolic space. Linear decision boundaries in hyperbolic space are a set of geodesics (curves) that are obtained by intersecting the hyperboloid $\mathbb{H}^n$ with an n-dimensional hyperplane ($\langle w, x\rangle_{n+1} = 0$) in the ambient space $\mathbb{R}^{n+1}$. Authors (Cho et al., 2018) formulate the optimization problem to solve maximum margin classification with linear decision boundaries in hyperbolic space as

$$\begin{aligned} \arg\min_{w \in \mathbb{R}^{n+1}} f(w) := -\frac{1}{2}\langle w, w\rangle_{n+1} + \\ C\sum_{j=1}^{m} \max(0, \sinh^{-1}(1) - \sinh^{-1}(y^{(j)}(\langle w, x^{(j)}\rangle_{n+1}))), \end{aligned} \tag{2}$$

which closely resembles the Euclidean version, where Euclidean inner products are replaced with Minkowski inner products. The parameter C in Eq. 2 controls the tradeoff between minimizing misclassification and maximizing margin. In all our experiments we use our own Python implementation [3] of Hyperbolic Linear SVM compatible with scikit-learn (Pedregosa et al., 2011), which we based on the official open source implementation in Matlab [4].

Link prediction with neural embeddings. The usual way to perform link prediction with neural embeddings Θ is to use them as some kind of representation of a link l_i between u and v. In Euclidean space, one could leverage the underlying vector space structure and come up with link representations, such as vector addition ($l_i := \Theta(u) + \Theta(v)$) and element-wise multiplication of vector elements (Grover and Leskovec, 2016). Once we fix our link representation method, we can train binary classifiers $f(l_i)$ to perform link prediction (i.e., $f(l_i) > 0.5$ if there is a link between u and v and $f(l_i) \leq 0.5$ otherwise). Such link representations may take into account more geometrical patterns than those that rely on the notion of distance alone (e.g., Fermi-Dirac distribution $P((u,v) = 1 \mid \Theta) = 1/(e^{(d(\Theta(u),\Theta(v))-r)/t} + 1)$ as in (Nickel and Kiela, 2017)).

Experimental setting. For each knowledge graph we perform a nested cross-validation procedure for 10 runs. In each run, first, we split independently positive links 10 times into train (80%) and test (20%) datasets. We further generate negative links for each split dataset with the positive to negative ratio 1:1 (i.e., both train and test datasets have this ratio). We then use positive links of the train dataset to compute neural embeddings in hyperbolic $\Theta_{\mathbb{H}^n}$ and Euclidean spaces $\Theta_{\mathbb{R}^n}$ by minimizing the loss function in Eq. 1. Note that we pre-train hyperbolic embeddings on flat graph-representations of knowledge graphs, i.e., all edges are unlabelled, and each pair is connected with at most one edge (the description of this pipeline in Euclidean space in (Agibetov and Samwald, 2018)). Next, we train separate binary classifiers for each relation type with Euclidean and hyperbolic SVM classifiers. Performance of binary classifiers is evaluated with the area under the receiver-operator curve (ROC AUC), and is averaged over all 10 runs. This nested cross-validation procedure with 10 runs is computed separately in Euclidean and hyperbolic cases for dimensions $d \in \{2, 5, 10\}$. For a fair comparison we train embeddings for 500 epochs each time. In both hyperbolic and Euclidean SVMs, the parameter $C \in \{0.1, 1, 10\}$ (Eq.2) is optimized separately on the training dataset for each run.

3 Results and discussion

Table 1 summarizes results of our experiments, where we compared the classification performance of Euclidean and hyperbolic embeddings in conjunction with Euclidean and hyperbolic large-margin classifiers. Each score in this table represents an average classification score of 10 nested cross-validation runs over all relations in the knowledge graph (each relation score itself is an average over 10 runs, and the final score is the average over all relations). Our comparisons are reported for a increasing number of dimensions

[1] https://github.com/lateral/geodesic-poincare-embeddings

[2] https://github.com/facebookresearch/StarSpace

[3] https://github.com/plumdeq/hsvm

[4] https://github.com/hhcho/hyplinear

	dim d	Euclidean embeddings		Hyperbolic embeddings	
		Euc SVM	Hyp SVM	Euc SVM	Hyp SVM
UMLS					
	2	0.661 ± 0.023	0.616 ± 0.019	0.695 ± 0.026	$\mathbf{0.703 \pm 0.018}$
	5	$\mathbf{0.780 \pm 0.023}$	0.743 ± 0.024	0.735 ± 0.030	0.743 ± 0.024
	10	$\mathbf{0.793 \pm 0.025}$	0.754 ± 0.022	0.767 ± 0.031	0.742 ± 0.026
BIO-KG					
	2	$\mathbf{0.692 \pm 0.010}$	0.691 ± 0.010	0.613 ± 0.006	0.676 ± 0.009
	5	$\mathbf{0.776 \pm 0.010}$	0.771 ± 0.011	0.697 ± 0.008	0.756 ± 0.011
	10	0.732 ± 0.009	0.723 ± 0.008	0.711 ± 0.010	$\mathbf{0.763 \pm 0.010}$

Table 1: Performance comparison of flat and curved embeddings and large-margin classifiers for biological link prediction task. Link prediction is performed by training large-margin classifiers in Euclidean (Euc SVM) and hyperbolic (Hyp SVM) spaces on Euclidean and hyperbolic embeddings (classifiers and embeddings are trained separately). Embeddings are trained once per graph, while one separate classifier is trained for each type of relation. Performance of a classifier to predict a link of a certain type is measured with ROC AUC score. Each cell represents a ROC AUC score ($\pm$ SD (standard deviation)) averaged over all relations in a graph (each relation ROC AUC score is itself averaged after a 10 fold cross-validation.

($d \in [2, 5, 10]$).

Results for UMLS confirmed the main hypothesis supported in (Nickel and Kiela, 2017; De Sa et al., 2018) that hyperbolic embeddings outperform Euclidean embeddings with fewer dimensions. And, as reported in (Cho et al., 2018), that large-margin classification in hyperbolic space utilizes the curved geometry of the learned embeddings better than its flat counterpart (linear euclidean SVM classifier). Moreover, the UMLS graph contains many links (e.g., PART OF) that inherently encode hierarchical semantic relations between the nodes, which are better represented in the hyperbolic space. However, as we increase the number of dimensions, Euclidean embeddings and Euclidean SVM outperform its hyperbolic competitors.

In case of a bigger and complex graph (BIO-KG) the situation seems to be the exact opposite – hyperbolic toolbox largely outperforms its Euclidean counterpart as we increase the size of dimensions ($d = 10$), while flat classifier and flat embeddings perform better with fewer dimensions ($d = 2, 5$). This could be due to the fact that 500 epochs are not enough to disentangle complex biological knowledge in the hyperbolic space in lower dimensions.

In all of our experiments Hyperbolic SVM had significantly better training performance (ROC AUC) than Euclidean SVM, which shows that the curved hyperbolic space does represent the training data better, however, has a poorer generalization trait than its Euclidean counterpart.

4 Lessons learned and future directions

The benefit of learning hyperbolic embeddings is that they require fewer dimensions to capture latent semantic and hierarchical information. This is important for scalability and interpretability (easier to visualize 2 or 3 dimensional embeddings).

From our preliminary results we observed that hyperbolic embeddings capture latent hierarchical semantic relations of the UMLS graph better than Euclidean embeddings in lower dimensions, similar to the state-of-the-art results for the reconstruction of hierarchical relationships (Nickel and Kiela, 2017, 2018; Ganea et al., 2018). For complex and big graphs, such as BIO-KG, we would recommend training hyperbolic embeddings for longer periods (> 500 epochs) in order to better disentangle complex information.

While training hyperbolic embeddings is notorious for long computational time, recent advances in Riemannian SGD optimization in hyperboloid model of hyperbolic space (Wilson and Leimeister, 2018) provide us with computational tools that run much faster than analogous approaches in Poincare ball model (Nickel and Kiela, 2017) (still much slower than in the Euclidean case). Finally, we believe that in order to learn better hyperbolic embeddings (and do it faster), the next steps should be focused on end-to-end hyperbolic embedding training, where hyperbolic large-margin classifier loss is directly incorporated during the training process.

References

Asan Agibetov and Matthias Samwald. 2018. Global and local evaluation of link prediction tasks with neural embeddings. *arXiv*.

Gregorio Alanis-Lobato, Pablo Mier, and Miguel A Andrade-Navarro. 2016. Efficient embedding of complex networks to hyperbolic space via their laplacian. *Sci Rep*, 6:30108.

Mona Alshahrani, Mohammad Asif Khan, Omar Maddouri, Akira R Kinjo, Nria Queralt-Rosinach, and Robert Hoehndorf. 2017. Neuro-symbolic representation learning on biological knowledge graphs. *Bioinformatics*, 33(17):2723–2730.

Olivier Bodenreider. 2004. The unified medical language system (UMLS): integrating biomedical terminology. *Nucleic Acids Res*, 32(Database issue):D267–70.

Benjamin Paul Chamberlain, James Clough, and Marc Peter Deisenroth. 2017. Neural embeddings of graphs in hyperbolic space. *arXiv:1705.10359 [cs, stat]*.

Hyunghoon Cho, Benjamin DeMeo, Jian Peng, and Bonnie Berger. 2018. Large-margin classification in hyperbolic space. *arXiv*.

Christopher De Sa, Albert Gu, Christopher R, and Frederic Sala. 2018. Representation tradeoffs for hyperbolic embeddings. *arXiv*.

N.V. Efimov. 1963. Impossibility of a complete regular surface in euclidean 3-space whose gaussian curvature has a negative upper bound. *Sov. Math. (Doklady)*, 4:843–846.

Octavian-Eugen Ganea, Gary Bcigneul, and Thomas Hofmann. 2018. Hyperbolic entailment cones for learning hierarchical embeddings. *arXiv*.

Aditya Grover and Jure Leskovec. 2016. node2vec: Scalable feature learning for networks. *KDD*, 2016:855–864.

Dmitri Krioukov, Fragkiskos Papadopoulos, Maksim Kitsak, Amin Vahdat, and Marin Bogu. 2010. Hyperbolic geometry of complex networks. *Phys Rev E Stat Nonlin Soft Matter Phys*, 82(3 Pt 2):036106.

Maximilian Nickel and Douwe Kiela. 2017. Poincaré embeddings for learning hierarchical representations. *arXiv:1705.08039 [cs, stat]*.

Maximilian Nickel and Douwe Kiela. 2018. Learning continuous hierarchies in the lorentz model of hyperbolic geometry. *arXiv*.

Maximilian Nickel, Kevin Murphy, Volker Tresp, and Evgeniy Gabrilovich. 2016. A review of relational machine learning for knowledge graphs. *Proc. IEEE*, 104(1):11–33.

Fabian Pedregosa, Gal Varoquaux, Alexandre Gramfort, Vincent Michel, Bertrand Thirion, Olivier Grisel, Mathieu Blondel, Peter Prettenhofer, Ron Weiss, Vincent Dubourg, Jake Vanderplas, Alexandre Passos, David Cournapeau, Matthieu Brucher, Matthieu Perrot, and Èdouard Duchesnay. 2011. Scikit-learn: Machine learning in python. *Journal of Machine Learning Research*.

S.N. Sri Nurdiati and C. Hoede. 2008. *25 years development of knowledge graph theory: the results and the challenge*. Number 2/1876 in Memorandum. Discrete Mathematics and Mathematical Programming (DMMP).

Benjamin Wilson and Matthias Leimeister. 2018. Gradient descent in hyperbolic space. *arXiv*.

Extending Neural Question Answering with Linguistic Input Features

Fabian Hommel[1] **Matthias Orlikowski**[1] **Philipp Cimiano**[1,2] **Matthias Hartung**[1]
[1]Semalytix GmbH, Bielefeld, Germany
[2]Semantic Computing Group, Bielefeld University, Germany
first.last@semalytix.com

Abstract

Considerable progress in neural question answering has been made on competitive general domain datasets. In order to explore methods to aid the generalization potential of question answering models, we reimplement a state-of-the-art architecture, perform a parameter search on an open-domain dataset and evaluate a first approach for integrating linguistic input features such as part-of-speech tags, syntactic dependency relations and semantic roles. The results show that adding these input features has a greater impact on performance than any of the architectural parameters we explore. Our findings suggest that these layers of linguistic knowledge have the potential to substantially increase the generalization capacities of neural QA models, thus facilitating cross-domain model transfer or the development of domain-agnostic QA models.

1 Introduction

Recently, deep neural network approaches for question answering (QA) have gained traction. The strong interest in this task may be explained by two promises that resonate in neural QA approaches: For one thing, QA is claimed to bear the potential to subsume a lot of other NLP challenges. From this perspective, almost every task can be framed as a natural language question (Kumar et al., 2016). Thus, a QA model with the capacity to learn mappings from natural language terminology to formal linguistic concepts could be used as a *surrogate model*, reducing annotation and training effort and providing fast solutions to potentially complex NLP problems. For another, QA systems have always been considered as intuitive natural language interfaces for *information access* in various domains of (technical) knowledge.

As any other practical NLP solution targeting specialized domains, QA systems face the inherent challenges of cross-domain generalization or domain adaptation, respectively. However, QA approaches can be considered particularly suitable for this kind of problem, as the semantic underpinnings of question/answer pairs capture a universal layer of meaning that is domain-agnostic to some extent (but might require fine-tuning wrt. particular domain concepts or terminology).

We hypothesize that a promising approach towards rapid information access in specialized domains would be (i) to learn the aforementioned universal meaning layer from large collections of open-domain question/answer pairs, and (ii) adapt the resulting meaning representations to more specific domains subsequently. In this paper, we focus on the first problem.

Our work is based on the assumption that rich representations of linguistic knowledge at high levels of syntactic and semantic abstraction facilitates neural NLP models to capture "universal", domain-agnostic meaning, which in turn fosters performance in open-domain QA. Against this backdrop, we evaluate the impact of explicitly encoded linguistic information in terms of part-of-speech tags, syntactic dependencies and semantic roles on open-domain performance of a state-of-the-art neural QA model. We find that our re-implementation of the deep neural QANet architecture (Yu et al., 2018) benefits considerably from these linguistically enriched representations, which we consider a promising first step towards generalizable, rapidly adaptable QA models.

2 Related Work

In recent years, research about feature engineering for NLP models has subsided to some extent. This might be attributed to the ability of neural networks to perform hierarchical feature learning

(Bengio, 2009). Using neural approaches, many of the core NLP tasks like part-of-speech (PoS) tagging (Koo et al., 2008), dependency parsing (Chen and Manning, 2014), named entity recognition (Lample et al., 2016) and semantic role labelling (Roth and Woodsend, 2014; Zhou and Xu, 2015) have been improved. However, recent papers that make use of the improved performance in these areas are few (Alexandrescu and Kirchhoff, 2006; Sennrich and Haddow, 2016). Thus, we want to evaluate whether adding linguistic information to the inputs of a QA model improves the performance. Our approach to integrating linguistic input features by embedding each individually and concatenating the embeddings is inspired by Sennrich and Haddow (2016), who apply this approach in the context of machine translation.

This paper builds upon a host of recent developments in neural architectures for question answering or reading comprehension. While most approaches rely heavily on recurrent layers (Huang et al., 2017; Hu et al., 2018; Seo et al., 2016; Shen et al., 2017; Wang et al., 2017; Xiong et al., 2016), we chose to reimplement QANet, a self-attention based architecture (Yu et al., 2018).

Apart from that, we use the tools from Roth and Woodsend (2014) for extracting semantic roles over the whole Stanford Question Answering Dataset (SQuAD) (Rajpurkar et al., 2016).

3 Extending QANet with Linguistic Input Features

As a testbed in order to assess the impact of linguistic input features in neural QA models, we make use of (a re-implementation of) QANet (Yu et al., 2018). By default, QANet solely uses word and character inputs. However, numerous off-the-shelf NLP tools are available that could be used to enrich these inputs with explicit linguistic information. This option is potentially interesting when trying to adapt a model to other domains: While additional training data might be expensive to obtain, these linguistic input features could boost the performance by providing a scalable, domain-agnostic source of information. We expand the per-word inputs with three different kinds of linguistic features: part-of-speech (PoS) tags, dependency relation labels and semantic roles.

PoS Tags. We hypothesized that the information about the part-of-speech of input tokens would help the neural network by reducing the number of answer candidates for specific types of questions. To extract POS tags for all contexts and questions, we used the coarse-graind PoS tag set of the spaCy library[1].

Dependency Relation Labels. We expected that syntactic information might help the model to predict the boundaries of spans with more precision. Again, we use spaCy to extract dependency information for questions and contexts. To extract dependency information per input word, we use the type label of that dependency relation in which the word is the child.

Semantic Roles. Semantic Role Labeling (SRL) deals with the problem of finding shallow semantic structure in sentences by identifying events ("predicates") and their participants ("semantic roles"). By identifying predicates and related participants and properties, SRL helps to answer "who" did "what" to "whom", "where", "when" and "how"? To do that, each constituent in a sentence is assigned a semantic role from a predifined set of roles like agent, patient or location (Márquez et al., 2008). Since semantic role labeling aims at identifying relevant aspects of events that are directly related to the above-mentioned WH questions, question answering models should directly benefit from this kinds of information.

We used the mate-plus tools (Roth and Woodsend, 2014) for parsing the complete SQuAD dataset and to obtain PropBank-labeled semantic roles per input word (Palmer et al., 2005). We added the role `<PREDICATE>` to the set of semantic roles to provide the model with pointers to the basic events. Words that did not correspond to any semantic role were assigned a `<NOROLE>` label.

Integration of Linguistic Features in QANet. In the standard QANet architecture, words and corresponding characters are embedded individually and then concatenated to obtain one representation vector per input word. Following Sennrich and Haddow (2016), we enrich this process by mapping each of the linguistic input features described above to its own embedding space and then including them into the concatenation. Figure 1 shows an updated version of the input embedding layer of QANet that includes the linguistic input features.

[1]Available at https://spacy.io/

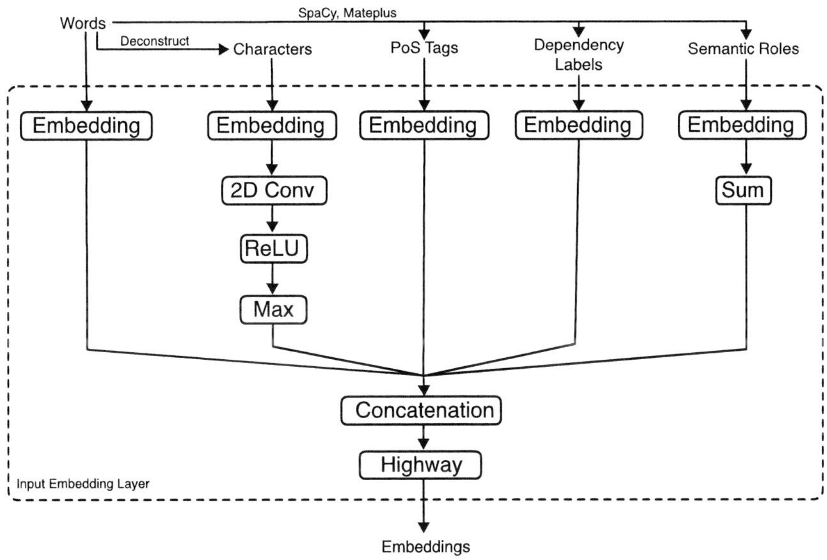

Figure 1: The low-level structure of the input embedding layer, enriched with additional linguistic inputs.

Each embedding vector consists of the embedded information of the word, its characters, its PoS tag, the label of the dependency relation in which the respective word is the child and its semantic roles. While the PoS tags and dependency relation labels are single word-level features and can be embedded by standard indexing and look-up, each word can have multiple semantic roles. Therefore, we embed each semantic role separately and aggregate over them. After preliminary experimentation with convolution, summing and taking the maximum, we decided for summing along each dimension of the semantic role embeddings[2]. This results in one aggregated semantic role embedding vector per input word. Note that we intentionally do not compute any combinations of the features mentioned above manually. We simply enrich the available word-level input information and rely on the network to find meaningful connections.

4 Experiments

To obtain a baseline, we reimplemented QANet and performed a parameter search. After that, we evaluated the integration of linguistic input features against that baseline.

4.1 Parameter Exploration in QANet

In the first experiment, we explore the effect of various parameters on open-domain QA performance in our re-implementation of QANet. The aim is to understand the impact of each parameter to compare it to the contribution of linguistic input features.

[2]We set the maximum of semantic roles per word to 8

Dataset. We use the Stanford Question Answering Dataset (SQuAD) (Rajpurkar et al., 2016) for parameter search. Yu et al. (2018) state that the results on development and test set are strongly correlated. Thus, improvements on the development set of SQuAD should also lead to improvements on the test set. Based on this claim, we only report results on the development set, since the test set of SQuAD is not publicly available. The training set consists of 87599 samples and the test set consists of 10570 samples. All texts are in English language.

Preprocessing. To preprocess SQuAD, we used the spaCy library for tokenization. We truncated or padded each paragraph to length 400 and each question to length 30. Each token was transformed into lower case and embedded using pre-trained GloVe (Pennington et al., 2014) embeddings. All words that were either out-of-vocabulary or not present at training time were mapped to a randomly initialized unknown token (<UNK>). For each token, we extracted all characters and then truncated or padded them to 16 characters per word. Each character embedding was initialized randomly.

Parameter	ΔF1	ΔEM
word embeddings	**2.4**	1.8
character embeddings	1.6	1.7
# convolutional layers	1.5	**2.2**
shared wheights in encoding	1.3	1.3
# encoder blocks	0.9	0.9
# attention heads	0.6	1.2
# highway layers	0.4	1.0
model dimensionalty	0.5	0.8
pointwise feed-forward layers	0.2	0.0
combination of best settings	1.7	1.9

Table 1: Impact of evaluated individual parameters and the combination of their best settings on F1 and exact match (EM) scores.

Training Parameters. For regularization, we adopted the methods from Yu et al. (2018): We apply L2 weight decay on all trainable variables with $\lambda = 3 \times 10^{-7}$ and dropout on word embeddings ($p = 0.1$), as well as on character embeddings ($p = 0.05$). Additionally, a dropout of rate 0.1 is applied on every layer except from the output layer. Apart from that, we employ the stochastic depth method (Huang et al., 2016) inside each stack of encoder blocks during training. In order to compute the probabilities p_l we use a linear decay rule: $p_l = 1 - \frac{l}{L}(1 - p_L)$, following Huang et al. (2016); Yu et al. (2018). L denotes the index of the last layer in a stack of encoder blocks and the corresponding probability p_L is set to 0.9.

As an optimizer, we use ADAM (Kingma and Ba, 2014) with $\beta_1 = 0.8$, $\beta_2 = 0.999$ and $\varepsilon = 10^{-7}$ (Yu et al., 2018). To prevent an exploding gradient, we use gradient norm clipping (Pascanu et al., 2013) with a threshold of 5. We use a learning rate warm-up schema with a logarithmic increase from 0.0 to 0.001 in the first 1000 gradient steps. After that, the learning rate is kept fixed at 0.001. Finally, we apply an exponential moving average with decay rate 0.9999 on all trainable variables. We implemented our model in PyTorch[3] (Paszke et al., 2017) and trained on a geforce GTX 1080 GPU with 12gb RAM.

Results. For evaluation, we use the F1 and exact match (EM) metrics from the official SQuAD evaluation script. See Table 1 for an overview of the impact of parameters on the scores.

Looking at the individual impact, the most influential parameters are the dimensionality of the inputs, namely the word and character embedding sizes. The parameter with the highest impact on F1 and the second highest impact on Exact Match is the word embedding size (ΔF1 = 2.4, ΔEM = 1.8). Surprisingly, the best setting is the smallest embedding size (50). In contrast, bigger character embedding sizes perform better than smaller ones. The best setting was a size of 300 (ΔF1 = 1.6, ΔEM = 1.7). Possibly, using no word embeddings at all and scaling up the character embeddings could increase the performance further and eliminate the need for pre-trained embeddings altogether. The most influential architectural parameter was the number of convolutional layers in model encoder blocks (ΔF1 = 1.5, ΔEM = 2.2), with the highest impact of all parameters on the exact match score when using 5 convolutional layers instead of 2. The second most influential structural parameter was sharing the weights between the embedding encoder layers for question and context (ΔF1 = 1.3, ΔEM = 1.3). The third most influential structural parameter was the number of encoder blocks in the model encoder layer, where 5 instead of 7 blocks yielded the best result (ΔF1 = 0.9, ΔEM = 0.9). The number of attention heads had a minor influence on F1 (ΔF1 = 0.6) but a notable influence on exact match (ΔEM = 1.2). Fortunately, these results are due to using only 2 attention heads. Thus, we propose to use less attention heads in order to improve results and reduce computational processing costs. The remaining parameters (the number of highway layers in the input embedding layer, the model dimensionality and the usage of pointwise feed-forward layers) all had negligible impacts on the performance. In general, we propose to set them to small values to reduce computational cost.

Combining the best settings for each parameter in isolation did not yield the best overall results in either F1 or exact match (ΔF1 = 1.7, ΔEM = 1.9). This combination was, however, the second best option for *both* F1 *and* exact match. Since this balanced quality was not apparent in any other setting, we decided to use this combination of parameters for all later experiments. The final performance of this baseline model was F1 = 67.8 and Exact Match = 55.5.

[3]pytorch.org

	F1	EM
Baseline	67.8	55.5
50d PoS embeddings	69.6	58.1
100d PoS embeddings	**69.7**	**58.9**
200d PoS embeddings	69.7	57.8
300d PoS embeddings	69.5	57.9
50d DL embeddings	68.6	56.6
100d DL embeddings	68.9	**57.8**
200d DL embeddings	67.8	56.6
300d DL embeddings	**69.0**	57.2
50d SRL embeddings	67.9	55.1
100d SRL embeddings	68.0	55.5
200d SRL embeddings	**68.8**	**56.6**
300d SRL embeddings	68.7	56.0

Table 2: Results of enriching the inputs with linguistic input embeddings of different sizes, in terms of F1 and exact match (EM) scores. DL refers to dependency labels, SRL to sematic role labels. No linguistic features were used in the baseline.

4.2 Impact of Linguistic Input Features

For evaluating the impact of linguistic input features, we used the same evaluation setup as for the baseline, including training data and meta-parameter choices. The embeddings for linguistic inputs were initialized randomly and then included as trainable parameters. Table 2 shows the results for varying the embedding dimensionality for each type of input feature, respectively, and also their combination.

PoS Tags. Adding PoS tags to the embedding space improves the overall performance of the network, regardless of the size of the embeddings. The best result is obtained by using PoS embeddings of size 100 ($\Delta F1 = 1.9, \Delta EM = 3.4$).

Dependency Relation Labels. Enriching the inputs with dependency relation information improves the overall performance. To achieve a strong improvement, the size of the embeddings matters: While embeddings of size 200 only improve the exact match ($\Delta F1 = 0.0, \Delta EM = 1.1$), all other sizes increase the F1 score as well. The biggest improvement in F1 score was achieved by an embedding size of 300 ($\Delta F1 = 1.2$), while the biggest improvement in EM score was achieved by an embedding size of 100 ($\Delta EM = 2.3$).

	F1	EM
Baseline (QANet Re-Impl.)	67.8	55.5
Baseline + Linguistic Inputs	**70.5**	**60.2**

Table 3: Results of using the combination of all three linguistic input features, using the previously optimized embedding sizes (PoS and dependency tags of size 100, semantic role labels of size 200). No linguistic features were used in the baseline setting.

Semantic Role Labels. Again, the linguistic inputs improve upon the baseline performance. However, in the setting with embedding size 50, the performance slightly deteriorates. The best performance is achieved when using embeddings of size 200 ($\Delta F1 = 1.0, \Delta EM = 1.1$).

Combination of all Linguistic Input Features. Table 3 shows the results for the combination of all three linguistic input features. The performance is the best in all our experiments, beating the previous baseline and individual linguistic input features ($\Delta F1 = 2.7, \Delta EM = 4.7$).

5 Discussion

Due to a gap in performance between our implementation of QANet (cf. Table 3) and the results from the original paper[4], we are not able to tell whether our optimized parameters are specific to our settings or should be preferred in general. The mismatch in performance could be due to various implementational differences (such as using PyTorch instead of Tensorflow), variation in preprocessing (e.g. tokenization with spaCy instead of NLTK) or the training procedure (such as trainable word embeddings). Still, we consider the relative improvements due to linguistic inputs compared to our baseline to be very insightful and promising.

Overall, each individual linguistic input achieved a small improvement of the performance. The best performing feature were the PoS embeddings, with the biggest improvements in both F1 and exact match ($\Delta F1 = 1.9, \Delta EM = 3.4$). The second best feature were the dependency relation labels ($\Delta F1 = 1.1, \Delta EM = 2.3$), followed by semantic role labels ($\Delta F1 = 1.0, \Delta EM = 1.1$). Combining all linguistic input features led to even better results ($\Delta F1 = 2.7, \Delta EM = 4.7$). This indicates that although the PoS tag embeddings

[4]F1=82.7, EM=73.6, as reported by Yu et al. (2018).

have the strongest impact on the performance, dependency relation and semantic role embeddings still provide useful additional information.

Importantly, this also shows that adding linguistic features into a model that incorporates optimally selected hyperparameters yields an additional performance benefit, suggesting that linguistic input features have a bigger impact on model performance than hyperparameter optimization alone. These findings underline the usefulness of linguistic features as a simple and readily available tool for enhancing the performance of QA models. Contrary to our intutions, the increase in performance seems to be lower in those features that are higher up in the hierarchy of linguistic abstraction: PoS tags, which merely provide a shallow and coarse-grained approximation of meaning, perform better than semantic roles, which provide a lot of information that should support the question answering task. This could be explained as follows: First, PoS tags (and dependency relation labels) are available for every word in a sentence, but only some words correspond to semantic roles. This sparsity renders this input feature less reliable. Second, our current aggregation approach towards semantic role embeddings might not be optimal.

The results suggest that syntactic information in dependency labels might help the model to find more precise boundaries: While the F1 score only increased by 1.1, the exact match was improved by 2.3. Even though the employed embedding process for the dependency labels was rather simple and not tailored to the underlying dependency tree structure, the feature was useful to the network. Probably, the performance of this feature could be increased either by classical feature engineering to construct more specific information from the dependency tree or by using a more suitable network architecture for embedding such structures.

Feature Engineering for Neural Architectures At least in higher-level tasks like QA, we observe a recent trend in the literature to focus on improving model architecture over improving input features, possibly due to the ability of neural networks to learn hierarchical features. Following this paradigm, the state-of-the-art in many tasks has recently been improved, for example in semantic role labeling through a deep highway BiLSTM (He et al., 2017). However, the last papers that make use of semantic roles are mostly from the last decade (Shen and Lapata, 2007; Kaisser and Webber, 2007; Sammons et al., 2009; Wu and Fung, 2009; Liu, 2009; Gao and Vogel, 2011). Most current QA architectures use word and character embeddings only (Seo et al., 2016; Wang et al., 2017; Xiong et al., 2016; Shen et al., 2017; Hu et al., 2018; Yu et al., 2018).

Our results suggest that the QANet model benefits more from better inputs than from optimizing its structure: When exploring the parameters, we observed that the embedding dimensionality of words and characters had the biggest impact. In the experiments regarding linguistic input features, we found that injecting linguistic information into the input had a stronger effect than any of the previously explored parameters.

Based on this, it might be worthwhile to invest more work into the investigation of the type of inputs one feeds into a neural model. An advantage of better inputs is their adaptability, since input features can possibly be used off-the-shelf for a wide range of tasks, while architectures typically have to be fine tuned on supervised training data. Another advantage might be that empirical gains are better interpretable: In our experiments, linguistic input features had a bigger impact on exact match (finding exact boundaries of the correct answer) than on F1 (overlap with correct answer). A thorough investigation of this intuitive link between input and output qualities would be necessary to support this claim.

6 Conclusion

This paper addresses the question as to whether neural QA models benefit from linguistic input features at different levels of abstraction in terms of their presumed generalization capacities across domains. To this end, we evaluate the impact of injecting different linguistic inputs (PoS tags, syntactic dependencies, semantic roles) into a deep neural QA architecture on open-domain performance over SQuAD, which constitutes the largest open-domain benchmark data set currently available.

In our experiments, the highest individual performance gain was achieved by adding PoS tags to the input representation, but a combination of all evaluated linguistic features led to the best results overall. We noticed that linguistic input features had a bigger impact on the exact match score than on the F1 score. Thus, we hypothesize that the linguistic information facilitates boundary detection, while locating answer candidates in general may largely depend on word-level semantics.

In future work, it might be instructive to explore how well linguistic features perform without word or character inputs. This would give a better basic intuition about the performance of each individual feature. Another interesting research direction could be to investigate further linguistic information like lemmatized words, subword tags and morphological features (Sennrich and Haddow, 2016), named entity recognition and distance and position features. Apart from that, novel approaches for integrating this information could be worthwhile: While features that have one value per word (like PoS tags) can be easily embedded, relational features or features with multiple values per word (like semantic roles) need some kind of aggregation. While we chose summing over individual dimensions, various other approaches like convolution, recurrent layers or even self-attention might lead to better results. Tree-structured features like dependency trees might benefit from recursive encoding layers (Socher et al., 2011).

We conclude that linguistic input features provide meaningful information to neural QA models and that they improve performance on a general domain dataset. In future, we plan to evaluate whether they might be employed for generalizing QA models to new specialized domains.

Acknowledgments

This work was supported in part by the H2020 project Prêt-à-LLOD under Grant Agreement number 825182.

References

Andrei Alexandrescu and Katrin Kirchhoff. 2006. Factored neural language models. In *Human Language Technology Conference of the North American Chapter of the Association of Computational Linguistics, Proceedings, June 4-9, 2006, New York, New York, USA*.

Yoshua Bengio. 2009. Learning deep architectures for AI. *Foundations and Trends in Machine Learning*, 2(1):1–127.

Danqi Chen and Christopher D. Manning. 2014. A fast and accurate dependency parser using neural networks. In *Proceedings of the 2014 Conference on Empirical Methods in Natural Language Processing, EMNLP 2014, October 25-29, 2014, Doha, Qatar, A meeting of SIGDAT, a Special Interest Group of the ACL*, pages 740–750.

Qin Gao and Stephan Vogel. 2011. Utilizing target-side semantic role labels to assist hierarchical phrase-based machine translation. In *Proceedings of Fifth Workshop on Syntax, Semantics and Structure in Statistical Translation, SSST@ACL 2011, Portland, Oregon, USA, 23 June, 2011*, pages 107–115.

Luheng He, Kenton Lee, Mike Lewis, and Luke Zettlemoyer. 2017. Deep semantic role labeling: What works and what's next. In *Proceedings of the 55th Annual Meeting of the Association for Computational Linguistics, ACL 2017, Vancouver, Canada, July 30 - August 4, Volume 1: Long Papers*, pages 473–483.

Minghao Hu, Yuxing Peng, Zhen Huang, Xipeng Qiu, Furu Wei, and Ming Zhou. 2018. Reinforced mnemonic reader for machine reading comprehension. In *Proceedings of the Twenty-Seventh International Joint Conference on Artificial Intelligence, IJCAI 2018, July 13-19, 2018, Stockholm, Sweden.*, pages 4099–4106.

Gao Huang, Yu Sun, Zhuang Liu, Daniel Sedra, and Kilian Q. Weinberger. 2016. Deep networks with stochastic depth. In *Computer Vision - ECCV 2016 - 14th European Conference, Amsterdam, The Netherlands, October 11-14, 2016, Proceedings, Part IV*, pages 646–661.

Hsin-Yuan Huang, Chenguang Zhu, Yelong Shen, and Weizhu Chen. 2017. Fusionnet: Fusing via fully-aware attention with application to machine comprehension. *CoRR*, abs/1711.07341.

Michael Kaisser and Bonnie Webber. 2007. Question answering based on semantic roles. In *Proceedings of the workshop on deep linguistic processing*, pages 41–48. Association for Computational Linguistics.

Diederik P. Kingma and Jimmy Ba. 2014. Adam: A method for stochastic optimization. *CoRR*, abs/1412.6980.

Terry Koo, Xavier Carreras, and Michael Collins. 2008. Simple semi-supervised dependency parsing. In *ACL 2008, Proceedings of the 46th Annual Meeting of the Association for Computational Linguistics, June 15-20, 2008, Columbus, Ohio, USA*, pages 595–603.

Ankit Kumar, Ozan Irsoy, Peter Ondruska, Mohit Iyyer, James Bradbury, Ishaan Gulrajani, Victor Zhong, Romain Paulus, and Richard Socher. 2016. Ask me anything: Dynamic memory networks for natural language processing. In *Proceedings of The 33rd International Conference on Machine Learning*, volume 48 of *Proceedings of Machine Learning Research*, pages 1378–1387, New York, New York, USA. PMLR.

Guillaume Lample, Miguel Ballesteros, Sandeep Subramanian, Kazuya Kawakami, and Chris Dyer. 2016. Neural architectures for named entity recognition. In *NAACL HLT 2016, The 2016 Conference of the North American Chapter of the Association for Computational Linguistics: Human Language Technologies, San Diego California, USA, June 12-17, 2016*, pages 260–270.

Tie-Yan Liu. 2009. Learning to rank for information retrieval. *Foundations and Trends in Information Retrieval*, 3(3):225–331.

Lluís Màrquez, Xavier Carreras, Kenneth C. Litkowski, and Suzanne Stevenson. 2008. Semantic role labeling: An introduction to the special issue. *Computational Linguistics*, 34(2):145–159.

Martha Palmer, Paul Kingsbury, and Daniel Gildea. 2005. The proposition bank: An annotated corpus of semantic roles. *Computational Linguistics*, 31(1):71–106.

Razvan Pascanu, Tomas Mikolov, and Yoshua Bengio. 2013. On the difficulty of training recurrent neural networks. In *Proceedings of the 30th International Conference on Machine Learning, ICML 2013, Atlanta, GA, USA, 16-21 June 2013*, pages 1310–1318.

Adam Paszke, Sam Gross, Soumith Chintala, Gregory Chanan, Edward Yang, Zachary DeVito, Zeming Lin, Alban Desmaison, Luca Antiga, and Adam Lerer. 2017. Automatic differentiation in pytorch. In *NIPS-W*.

Jeffrey Pennington, Richard Socher, and Christopher D. Manning. 2014. Glove: Global vectors for word representation. In *Proceedings of the 2014 Conference on Empirical Methods in Natural Language Processing, EMNLP 2014, October 25-29, 2014, Doha, Qatar, A meeting of SIGDAT, a Special Interest Group of the ACL*, pages 1532–1543.

Pranav Rajpurkar, Jian Zhang, Konstantin Lopyrev, and Percy Liang. 2016. Squad: 100, 000+ questions for machine comprehension of text. In *Proceedings of the 2016 Conference on Empirical Methods in Natural Language Processing, EMNLP 2016, Austin, Texas, USA, November 1-4, 2016*, pages 2383–2392.

Michael Roth and Kristian Woodsend. 2014. Composition of word representations improves semantic role labelling. In *Proceedings of the 2014 Conference on Empirical Methods in Natural Language Processing, EMNLP 2014, October 25-29, 2014, Doha, Qatar, A meeting of SIGDAT, a Special Interest Group of the ACL*, pages 407–413.

Mark Sammons, V. G. Vinod Vydiswaran, Tim Vieira, Nikhil Johri, Ming-Wei Chang, Dan Goldwasser, Vivek Srikumar, Gourab Kundu, Yuancheng Tu, Kevin Small, Joshua Rule, Quang Do, and Dan Roth. 2009. Relation alignment for textual entailment recognition. In *Proceedings of the Second Text Analysis Conference, TAC 2009, Gaithersburg, Maryland, USA, November 16-17, 2009*.

Rico Sennrich and Barry Haddow. 2016. Linguistic input features improve neural machine translation. In *Proceedings of the First Conference on Machine Translation, WMT 2016, colocated with ACL 2016, August 11-12, Berlin, Germany*, pages 83–91.

Min Joon Seo, Aniruddha Kembhavi, Ali Farhadi, and Hannaneh Hajishirzi. 2016. Bidirectional attention flow for machine comprehension. *CoRR*, abs/1611.01603.

Dan Shen and Mirella Lapata. 2007. Using semantic roles to improve question answering. In *EMNLP-CoNLL 2007, Proceedings of the 2007 Joint Conference on Empirical Methods in Natural Language Processing and Computational Natural Language Learning, June 28-30, 2007, Prague, Czech Republic*, pages 12–21.

Yelong Shen, Po-Sen Huang, Jianfeng Gao, and Weizhu Chen. 2017. Reasonet: Learning to stop reading in machine comprehension. In *Proceedings of the 23rd ACM SIGKDD International Conference on Knowledge Discovery and Data Mining, Halifax, NS, Canada, August 13 - 17, 2017*, pages 1047–1055.

Richard Socher, Cliff Chiung-Yu Lin, Andrew Y. Ng, and Christopher D. Manning. 2011. Parsing natural scenes and natural language with recursive neural networks. In *Proceedings of the 28th International Conference on Machine Learning, ICML 2011, Bellevue, Washington, USA, June 28 - July 2, 2011*, pages 129–136.

Wenhui Wang, Nan Yang, Furu Wei, Baobao Chang, and Ming Zhou. 2017. Gated self-matching networks for reading comprehension and question answering. In *Proceedings of the 55th Annual Meeting of the Association for Computational Linguistics, ACL 2017, Vancouver, Canada, July 30 - August 4, Volume 1: Long Papers*, pages 189–198.

Dekai Wu and Pascale Fung. 2009. Semantic roles for SMT: A hybrid two-pass model. In *Human Language Technologies: Conference of the North American Chapter of the Association of Computational Linguistics, Proceedings, May 31 - June 5, 2009, Boulder, Colorado, USA, Short Papers*, pages 13–16.

Caiming Xiong, Victor Zhong, and Richard Socher. 2016. Dynamic coattention networks for question answering. *CoRR*, abs/1611.01604.

Adams Wei Yu, David Dohan, Minh-Thang Luong, Rui Zhao, Kai Chen, Mohammad Norouzi, and Quoc V. Le. 2018. Qanet: Combining local convolution with global self-attention for reading comprehension. *CoRR*, abs/1804.09541.

Jie Zhou and Wei Xu. 2015. End-to-end learning of semantic role labeling using recurrent neural networks. In *Proceedings of the 53rd Annual Meeting of the Association for Computational Linguistics and the 7th International Joint Conference on Natural Language Processing of the Asian Federation of Natural Language Processing, ACL 2015, July 26-31, 2015, Beijing, China, Volume 1: Long Papers*, pages 1127–1137.

How to Use Gazetteers for Entity Recognition with Neural Models

Simone Magnolini[1], **Valerio Piccioni**[1,2], **Vevake Balaraman**[1,2], **Marco Guerini**[1], **Bernardo Magnini**[1]
[1] Fondazione Bruno Kessler, Via Sommarive 18, Povo, Trento — Italy
[2] University of Trento, Italy.
{magnolini, balaraman, guerini, magnini}@fbk.eu
valerio.piccioni@studenti.unitn.it

Abstract

Although the use of end-to-end neural architectures has been proven to be effective on several sequence labeling tasks, the use of gazetteers in these architectures is still rather unexplored. We investigate several options, aiming at exploiting gazetteers to extract relevant features, and then at integrating these features in a neural model for entity recognition. We provide experimental evidences on two datasets (named entities and nominal entities) and two languages (English and Italian), showing that extracting features from a rich model of the gazetteer and then concatenating such features with the input embeddings of a neural model is the best strategy in all our experimental settings, significantly outperforming more conventional approaches.

1 Introduction

In the recent years a number of neural architectures have been successfully applied to several sequence labelling tasks, including, among others, part-of-speech tagging (Choi, 2016), named entity recognition (Ma and Hovy, 2016), and semantic role labeling (He et al., 2017). It has been shown that these architectures can achieve state-of-art performance with an end-to-end configuration, i.e. without recurring either to linguistic features or to external knowledge sources (e.g. gazetteers). However, experiments have been often conducted over datasets with large amount of training data and in a rather limited spectrum of experimental conditions. Overall, we think that there has not been much discussion about the use of gazetteers together with neural models, and that a deeper investigation is necessary.

In this paper we focus on the role of gazetteers for entity recognition. The following are our two main research questions: (i) As neural networks architectures are highly modular, which is the best way to integrate information from gazetteers? (ii) What is the impact of the size of both training data and gazetteers over the performance of a neural model for entity recognition?

As mentioned, we focus on entity recognition and refer to the Automatic Content Extraction program - ACE (Doddington et al., 2004). In this context, entity recognition has been approached as a sequence labeling task. Given an utterance $U = \{t_1, t_2, ..., t_n\}$ and a set of entity categories $C = \{c_1, c_2, ..., c_m\}$, the task is to label the tokens in U that refer to entities belonging to the categories in C. As an example, using the IOB format (Inside-Outside-Beginning, (Ramshaw and Marcus, 1995)), the sentence "I would like to order a salami pizza and two mozzarella cheese sandwiches" could be labeled as shown in Table 1. ACE distinguishes two main entity classes: *named entities* and *nominal entities*, and we consider both of them for our experiments.

The first entity class, named entities, roughly corresponds to proper names, and named entities recognition (NER) tools for frequent categories (i.e. persons as "Barack Obama", locations as "New York", and organizations as "IBM") have been developed for many languages. Several datasets are available for training purposes (e.g. the Conll-2003 datasets (Tjong Kim Sang and De Meulder, 2003)). It has been a common practice of NER systems to make use of gazetteers (i.e. lists of entity names), considering the presence of a token in certain gazetteer as an additional feature for the classifier (see, for instance, the use of the Stanford NER $useGazettes$ parameter for the CRF classifier (Finkel et al., 2005)).

Nominal entities, on the other hand, are noun phrase expressions describing an entity. Differently from named entities, nominal entities are typically compositional, as they do allow morphological and syntactic variations (e.g. for food

I	would	like	to	order	a	salami	pizza	and	two	mozzarella	cheese	sandwiches
O	O	O	O	O	O	B-FOOD	I-FOOD	O	O	B-FOOD	I-FOOD	I-FOOD

Table 1: IOB annotation of food entities inside user request.

names, *spanish baked salmon*, *roasted salmon* and *hot smoked salmon*), which makes it possible to combine tokens of one entity name with tokens of another entity name to generate new names (e.g. for food names, *salmon tacos* is a potential food name given the existence of *salmon* and *tacos*). In the framework of the ACE program there have been several attempts to develop supervised systems for nominal entities (Biggio et al., 2010); these systems, however, had to face the problem of the scarcity of annotated data, and, for this reason, were developed for few entity types.

In this paper we make use of an end-to-end state-of-art entity recognition system (described in Section 2), and investigate the combination with gazetteers under several integration methods, which are described in Section 3 and 4. Datasets for our experiments are described in Section 5, while results are presented and discussed in Section 6.

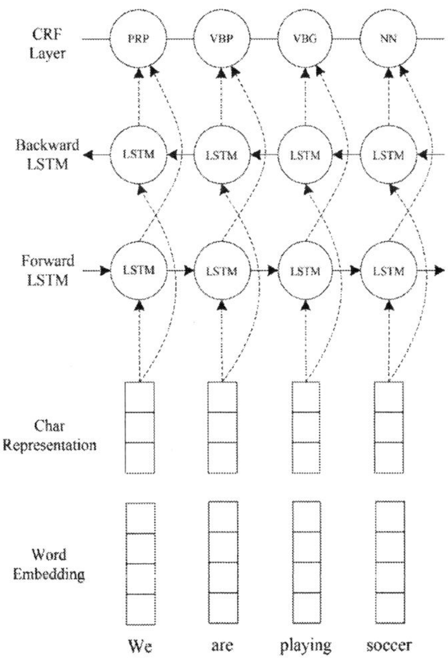

Figure 1: The main NeuroNLP2 structure. Dashed arrows indicate dropout layers applied on both the input and output vectors of BLSTM.

2 Core Entity Recognition System

In order to investigate the use of gazetteers in combination with neural models we first need an entity recognition system. For our experiments we have adopted the neural system proposed in (Ma and Hovy, 2016), which achieved state-of-art performance for named entity recognition for English on the ConLL-2003 dataset (see section 5). Specifically, we use the most recent implementation of the system in Pytorch distributed by the authors[1], and called *NeuroNLP2*. The system is composed of three layers (Figure 1): (i) a CNN that allows to extract information from the input text without any pre-processing; (ii) a bidirectional LSTM layer that presents each sequence forwards and backwards to two separate LSTM; (iii) a CRF layer that decodes the best label sequence.

For each token in the input sequence, first a character-level representation is computed by a CNN with character embeddings as inputs. Then the character-level representation vector is concatenated with the word embedding vector to feed the BLSTM network. The CNN for Character-level Representation is an effective approach to extract morphological information (like the prefix or suffix of a word) from characters of words and encode it into neural representations. In NeuroNLP2 the CNN is similar to the one proposed in (Chiu and Nichols, 2015), except that it uses only character embeddings as inputs, without character type.

At the second layer each input sequence is presented both forwards and backwards to a bidirectional LSTM, whose output allows to capture past and future information. LSTMs (Hochreiter and Schmidhuber, 1997) are variants of recurrent neural networks (RNNs) designed to cope with gradient vanishing problems. The LSTMs hidden state takes information only from the past, knowing nothing about the future. However, for many tasks it is beneficial to have access to both past (left) and future (right) contexts. A possible solution, whose effectiveness has been proven by previous work (Dyer et al., 2015), is provided by bi-directional LSTMs (BLSTM). (Ma and Hovy, 2016) apply a dropout layer on both the input and output vectors

[1] https://github.com/XuezheMax/NeuroNLP2

of the BLSTM.

Finally, the third layer implemented by NeuroNLP2 is a Conditional Random Fields (CRF) based decoder, which considers dependencies between entity labels in their context and then jointly decodes the best chain of labels for a given input sentence. For example, in NER with standard IOB annotation, an I-token can not follow an O, a constraint which is captured by the CFR layer. Conditional Random Fields (Lafferty et al., 2001) offer several advantages over hidden Markov models and stochastic grammars for such tasks, including the ability to relax strong independence assumptions made in those models. For a sequence CRF model (only interactions between two successive labels are considered), training and decoding can be solved efficiently by adopting the Viterbi algorithm.

We use exactly the same network parameters described in (Ma and Hovy, 2016) and provided as default by the available implementation. As input embeddings we use Stanford's publicly available GloVe 100-dimensional embeddings trained on 6 billion words from Wikipedia and web texts for English (in the same way as (Ma and Hovy, 2016)); for Italian we use Stanford's GloVe 50-dimensional embeddings trained on a Wikipedia's dump [2] with the default setup. For the out of vocabulary words we use a unique randomly generated vector for every word.

3 Gazetteers as Features

In this section we present three methods that allow us to exploit information contained in gazetteers and to represent such information as features to be used by the neural entity recognition system. While the first two methods, single token presence and multi-token presence, have been often used, the third method, i.e. gazetteer neural model, is based on the assumption that a more complex model can better exploit the properties of nominal entities.

3.1 Single Token Presence

A simple and straight-forward approach to use a gazetteer is to consider the presence of a single token in the gazetteer as a feature. To do that, we extract the vocabulary of the gazetteer and provide a boolean value to every token in the sentence, which indicates the presence or absence of the token in the vocabulary. If the number of gazetteers in the domain is n, corresponding to the number of entity classes, a single token takes a vector of n-dimensions: if the vocabularies of the different gazetteers do not overlap this is a one-hot vector, otherwise we can have multiple positive dimensions.

[2] 20/04/2018

3.2 Multi-token Presence

The second approach uses the same feature space as the single token presence method, but instead of checking for the presence of a single token in the gazetteer, it looks for the longest entity name in the gazetteer contained in the sentence. Let us consider the example in Table 1, *I would like to order a salami pizza and two mozzarella cheese sandwiches*, and assume a gazetteer for the class `FOOD` composed of two entries: *mozzarella pizza* and *salami sandwiches*. With the multi-token approach none of the tokens would have the gazetteer feature equal to true, while with the single token approach both *salami*, *pizza*, *mozzarella* and *sandwiches* would have the presence set to true. The multi-token technique enables a more consistent usage of gazetteers, especially in case of noisy entity names, although a possible drawback could be a lack of generalization.

3.3 Gazetteer Neural Model: NN$_g$

The third method to extract features from a gazetteer follows the intuition that the presence-absence approaches presented in Sections 3.1 and 3.2 might not be adequate for nominal entities, which show higher linguistic complexity than named entities. The idea is to build a neural classifier trained solely on gazetteers, that classifies a subsequence of tokens on the input sentence as belonging to a certain entity class with a certain confidence. Then we use the output of such classifier as a feature to be integrated within the NeuroNLP2 system.

The neural architecture of the entity classifier, the features it uses, and the methodology to generate synthetic negative examples are briefly presented in the following.

Architecture of the NN$_g$ Classifier. We used the neural gazetteer-based approach (called NN$_g$) proposed by (Guerini et al., 2018). The NN$_g$ classifier is implemented using a multilayer bidirectional LSTM that classifies an input sequence of

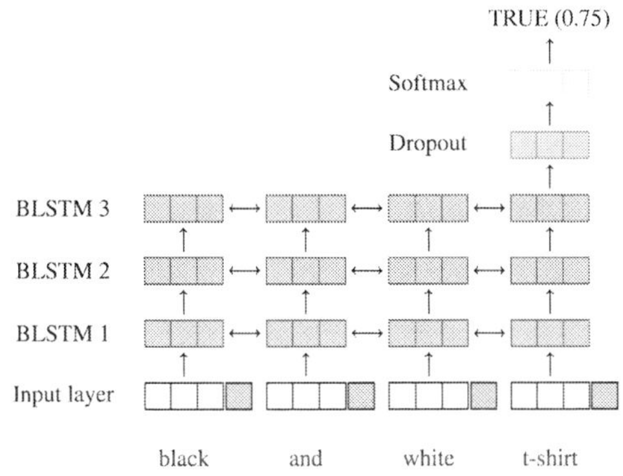

Figure 2: Structure of the neural gazetteer entity recognition (NN_g). The input layer concatenates the features in a single vector.

tokens either as an entity of a certain gazetteer or a non-entity, with a degree of confidence, i.e. the system classifies the sequences in number-of-gazetteers plus one (non-entity) different classes. The NN_g classifier is based on the system proposed in (Lample et al., 2016). The core is still a bidirectional LSTM, but it has a 3-layer BLSTM with 128 units per layer and with a single dropout layer (with a dropout probability of 0.5) between the third BLSTM and the output layer (a softmax layer). The topology of the network is depicted in Figure 2.

NN_g Classifier Features. The NN_g classifier combines several features: word embeddings, char-based embedding, and nine handcrafted features. Word embeddings are similar to those used for NeuroNLP2. For English we used Stanfords publicly available 50-dimensions embeddings, while for Italian we use 50-dimensional embeddings trained on a Wikipedia's dump with the default setup. The char-based embeddings, with a dimension of 30, are based on (Lample et al., 2016), and are trained on the entries in the gazetteers. The expected role of the char-based embeddings is to deal with out of vocabulary terms and possible word misspellings.

The handcrafted features are meant to explicitly represent the structure of a certain entity name, as it can be induced from the gazetteer in which the entity appears. NN_g considers nine features for each token in an entity name: (i) the actual position of the token within an entity name; (ii) the length of the entity name under inspection; (iii) the frequency of the token in the gazetteer; (iv) the average length of the entity names containing a certain token; (v) the average position of the token in the entity names it appears in; (vi) the bigram probability with reference to the previous token in the entity name; (vii) whether the token can be an entity or not; (viii) the ratio of the times the token is the first token in an entity name; (ix) the ratio of the times the token is the last token in an entity name.

Generating Synthetic Training Data. The NN_g classifier for a certain entity class is trained with both positive examples, i.e. entity names present in a gazetteer of the entity class, and negative examples, which are obtained by synthetic generation from the positive examples. In the following we explain how negative examples are generated.

For each entity name i in a gazetteer G (i.e. the positive example), negative counterparts are subsequences of i, or i with additional tokens at the beginning or end of it (or both), e.g. $t1 + i + t2$. Where $t1$ is the ending token of a random entity in G and $t2$ is the starting token of a random entity in G. Between these tokens and i there can be separators, as a white space, a comma or the *and* conjunction, so to mimic how multiple entities are usually expressed in sentences. Alternatively, $t1$ and $t2$ can be tokens randomly extracted from a generic corpus, so to mimic cases when the entity is expressed in isolation.

For example, if the initial positive example is *Community of Madrid*, the possible negative subsequences that are generated are: | *Community* | *of* | *Community of* | *of Madrid* |. The subsequence | *Madrid* | is not considered because it is already included in the gazetteer as positive example. Adding tokens, using the pattern $t1 + i + t2$, we obtain other potential negative examples: | *contemporary Community of Madrid* | *Community of Madrid and Murcia* | *contemporary Community of Madrid and Murcia* |, and so on. According to this procedure, we generate more negative examples than positive. In order to avoid a too unbalanced datatset, we randomly selected two negative examples for each positive example: a sub-sequence and an example surrounded by other words, resulting in a $1:2$ proportion.

4 Integrating Gazetteer Features

In this section we present the two methods used in our experiments to integrate the features extracted from gazetteers (see Section 3) into NeuroNLP2, the neural entity recognition system. Each of the integration methods adds one boolean feature for each gazetteer.

4.1 Integration 1: Gazetteer Features as Embedding Dimensions

Once we have extracted gazetteer features for each token of the input sentence, the first approach that we consider is to feed such features directly into the neural network. In this method the gazetteer information, represented by a n-dimensions vector, is simply concatenated with the embedding of each token of the input sentence. By default, the NeuroNLP2 system (see Section 2) uses both character and word embeddings, which are concatenated and passed on to the BLSTM layer to learn from them. In this approach the gazetteer feature is concatenated with the character and word embedding, and then it is passed to the BLSTM. The embedding representation for a given token x is as follows:

$$Embedding_x = [x_{word}; x_{char}; x_{gaz}]$$

While the integration as embedding dimensions for the single token and the multi-token features is straightforward, in order to combine NN_g with NeuroNLP2 we need to substitute part of the NN_g's network after training. In fact, we need a NN_g's output for every token, while NN_g classifies a sequence of tokens. To do that we remove the softmax layer of NN_g and we feed the output vectors of the third BLSTM to a fully connected layer of 32 nodes followed by a rectified linear unit (ReLU). With this modification we add to NeuroNLP2 32 features that represent a model of the gazetteers.

4.2 Integration 2: Gazetteer Features as Input for the CRF Classifier

As NER is a classification task, the system uses features extracted by the BLSTM layer to classify the tokens as one of the possible entity types. CRF is the probabilistic model adopted by NeuroNLP2 to classify a token with an entity type based on the features extracted. Providing the information of the gazetteer to this layer should help the model to better classify tokens. So this integration technique uses the gazetteer features as an additional dimension by concatenating them with the features extracted by the BLSTM.

CoNLL-2003				
	tokens	types	entities	sentences
Train	204567	23624	23499	14987
Dev	51578	9967	5942	3466
Test	46666	9489	5648	3684
DPD				
	tokens	types	entities	sentences
Train	4748	636	1757	450
Dev	296	138	122	49
Test	2315	379	583	200

Table 2: Statistics about data sets used for our experiments.

	dev ∩ train	test ∩ train	test ∩ gazetteers
CoNLL-2003	50%	35%	35%
DPD	48%	26%	33%

Table 3: Unique entities overlap between various sets. The percentage refers to the count of unique entities in the first dataset.

An example of this integration methodology applied to the features provided by the NN_g classifier is presented in Figure 3. It is important to notice that, like in the previous integration approach, NN_g is pre-trained and it is not jointly trained with NeuroNLP2.

5 Data Sets

In this section we describe the two datasets and the various gazetteers used for our experiments. The first dataset is CoNLL-2003 (Tjong Kim Sang and De Meulder, 2003), for named entity recognition, while the second one is a novel dataset (DPD) (Magnini et al., 2018), specifically focused on nominal entities. In Table 2 we report the main characteristics of the two datasets and the partitions used for the experiments, while in Table 3 we report the intersection among entities in the various sets (e.g. how many entities in the test set can be also found in the training set or the gazetteers). These percentages are a rough indicator of: (i) how a perfect match baseline using gazetteers can perform, and (ii) how much the NeuroNLP2 system can take advantage of already seen entities during training phase.

We describe the two datasets with more detail in the following two paragraphs.

CoNLL-2003 is a dataset specifically devoted to named entities: persons, locations, organizations and names of miscellaneous entities that do not belong to the previous three groups. While the data set comes in two languages (English and German) in this work we focus on English, whose

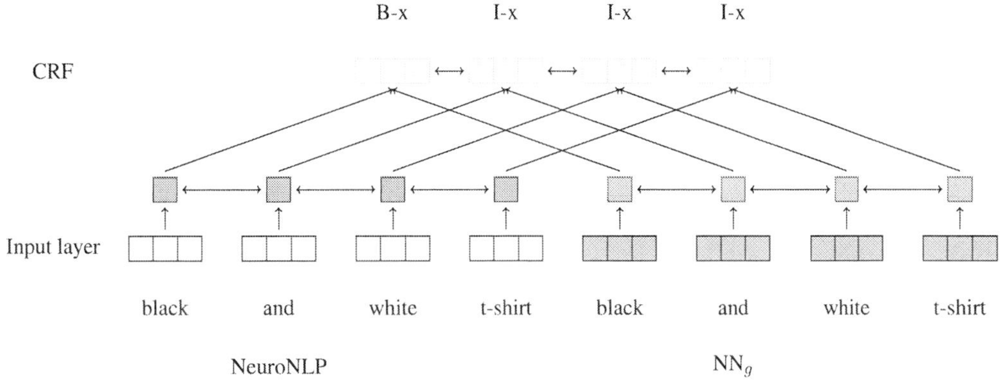

Figure 3: NeuroNLP + NN_g - the output layer of the two systems is combined into the CRF layer. For NN_g, a fully connected layer with 32 nodes and a ReLU has been substituted for the original SoftMax layer (in red).

data was taken from the Reuters news corpus. For instance, the sentence "EU rejects German call to boycott British lamb" is tagged as follows in CoNLL-2003:

<EU>$_{ORG}$ rejects <German>$_{MISC}$ call to boycott <British>$_{MISC}$ lamb.

DPD – Diabetic Patients Diary – is a data set in Italian made of diary entries of diabetic patients. Each day the patient has to write down what s/he ate in order to keep track of his/her dietary behavior. In this data set, which is much smaller than CoNNL-2003, all entities of type FOOD have been manually annotated by two annotators (inter-annotator agreement is 96.75 dice coefficient). Sentences in the dataset have a telegraphic style, e.g. the main verb is often missing, resulting in a list of foods like the following:

"<risotto ai multicereali e zucchine>$_{FOOD}$ <insalata>$_{FOOD}$ e <pomodori>$_{FOOD}$" ("<risotto with multigrain and zucchini> <salad> and <tomatoes>").

Entity Gazetteers. In Table 4 we describe the gazetteers that we have used in our experiments for the two datasets, reporting, for each entity type, sizes in terms of number of entity names, the average length of the names (in number of tokens), plus the length variability of such names (standard deviation). We also report additional metrics that try to grasp the complexity of entities names in the gazetteer: (i) the normalized type-token ratio (TTR), as a rough measure of how much lexical diversity is in the nominal entities in a gazetteer, see (Richards, 1987); (ii) the ratio of type1 tokens, i.e. tokens that can appear in the first position of an entity name but also in other positions, and type2 tokens, i.e. tokens appearing at the end and elsewhere; (iii) the ratio of entities that contain another entity as sub-part of their name. With these measures we are able to partially quantify how difficult it is to recognize the length of an entity (SD), how difficult it is to individuate the boundaries of an entity (ratio of type1 and type2 tokens), how much compositionality there is starting from basic entities (i.e. how many new entities can be potentially constructed by adding new tokens - sub-entity ratio). Note that type1 and type2 ratios can cover some cases in common with sub-entity ratio, but they model different phenomena: given *white t-shirt*, the entity name *black and white skirt* represents a case of type1 token for *white* but without sub-entity matching, while *white t-shirt with long sleeves* represents a sub-entity matching without making *white* a type1 token.

6 Experiments

The experimental results for the various approaches that use gazetteers as features in the context of a neural entity recognition system, are discussed in this Section. For all experiments, the hyper-parameters of the neural model for both NN_g and NeuroNLP2 are the same as in (Guerini et al., 2018) and (Ma and Hovy, 2016) respectively.

6.1 Overall Results

Tables 5 and 6 show the results of gazetteer integration as embedding and as CRF features, respectively. The NeuroNLP2 model benefits significantly from the gazetteer representation of NN_g, especially for the DPD dataset (with an increment of 2.54 in terms of F1). The combination of Neu-

Data Set	Gaz.	#entities	#tokens	length ± SD	TTR	type1(%)	type2(%)	sub-entity(%)
CoNNL	PER	3613	6454	1.79 ±0.54	0.96	19.00	04.63	23.60
	LOC	1331	1720	1.29 ±0.69	0.97	04.66	04.33	10.14
	ORG	2401	4659	1.94 ±1.16	0.91	09.35	15.06	19.44
	MISC	869	1422	1.64 ±0.94	0.89	08.61	08.73	19.85
DPD	FOOD	23472	83264	3.55 ±1.87	0.75	17.22	22.97	11.27

Table 4: Gazetteers used in the experiments. Description is provided in terms of number of entity names, total number of tokens, average length and standard deviation (SD) of entities, type-token ratio (norm obtained by repeated sampling of 200 tokens), type1 and type2 unique tokens ratio and sub-entity ratio.

	CoNLL				DPD			
	Accuracy	Precision	Recall	F1	Accuracy	Precision	Recall	F1
NeuroNLP2	98.06	91.42	90.95	91.19	88.47	77.17	74.79	75.96
NeuroNLP2 + single token	98.06	91.53	90.51	91.02	88.29	75.63	77.19	76.40
NeuroNLP2 + multi token	98.08	91.41	90.76	91.08	88.98	78.90	76.33	77.59
NeuroNLP2 + NN_g	98.05	91.41	91.02	**91.22**	89.89	79.68	77.36	**78.50**

Table 5: Experimental results using gazetteers as features together with embeddings.

roNLP2 and NN_g reaches state-of-art performance on ConNLL-2003 when it is added as embedding feature, while both the single token and the multi-token approaches do not improve the overall results. It can also be clearly seen that providing the gazetteer feature to CRF is a deteriorating choice, as the model probably tends to over-fit to the gazetteer information resulting in a drop of performance. On the other hand, using gazetteer features as part of embedding dimensions helps the model to adapt better when the training data are very few, like in the DPD dataset. Furthermore, the results on the DPD dataset of NeuroNLP2 + NN_g, compared to the others, show that NN_g correctly generalizes nominal entities from the gazetteer, improving both Recall and Precision with respect to the multi-token approach.

6.2 Impact of Training Size

Neural network architectures are data-hungry models, requiring large amounts of training data in order to generalize. In those scenarios where the amount of available training is not an issue the effect of the gazetteer on the model performance is negligible, as the model learns to generalize on the large number of annotated sentences. However, for domains where there is scarcity of training data, the gazetteer feature is much appreciated for a better performance. To understand this effect, we simulated a low data scenario for the CONLL-2003 dataset by training the model on a small amount of data. The test and dev datasets are kept the same, while varying only the training data size. Tables 7 and 8 show the performance of the models with varying training data sizes on CONLL and DPD datasets, respectively. We can infer that for Named Entity Recognition using token presence is not the right approach especially when the gazetteer is well formed and with little noise. The multi-token feature approach is more consistent, and it improves the performance of the NeuroNLP2 model by at least 3 points over all data sizes used. However, these approaches tend to be inconsistent when learning nominal entities. Results show that NN_g proves to be more robust for nominal entities and provides a more consistent performance indicating its impact in recognizing compositional entities. We can see that, for nominal entities, the single token approach is not recommended, as both the learning curve and the gazetteer size effect show (see Table 9).

Results are variable particularly for food names, which are nominal entities that can considerably change in length, contain stop-words, numbers or nouns that usually can appear in other contexts (i.e. *Miami beach* cocktail, *chinese* chicken, *white* wine, *pad* thai, *energy* balls...).

6.3 Impact of Gazetteer Size

In this section we investigate the impact of reducing the number of entities in the gazetteer, based on a "less common" principle, i.e. removing rare, but numerous, entries. As we can see in Table 9, the single token approach does not work well on food nominal entities, giving variable and unreliable results. In addition, removing entries that

	CoNLL				DPD			
	Accuracy	Precision	Recall	F1	Accuracy	Precision	Recall	F1
NeuroNLP2	98.06	91.42	90.95	91.19	88.47	77.17	74.79	75.96
NeuroNLP2 + single token	94.82	86.90	71.03	78.17	85.75	69.79	68.95	69.37
NeuroNLP2 + multi token	92.20	85.44	59.24	69.97	87.52	74.23	74.61	74.42
NeuroNLP2 + NN_g	97.96	90.95	90.53	90.74	89.37	78.56	74.79	**76.63**

Table 6: Experimental results using gazetteers as features for CRF.

	Data Size			
	100	200	300	450
NeuroNLP2	47.31	56.78	56.96	69.55
NeuroNLP2 + single token	47.70	59.25	61.32	71.66
NeuroNLP2 + multi token	**51.24**	**62.77**	**63.19**	**74.63**
NeuroNLP2 + NN_g	42.30	57.99	58.65	69.20

Table 7: Learning Curve on the CONLL 2003 dataset. Columns report the number of sentences in the training dataset.

	Data Size			
	100	200	300	450
NeuroNLP2	55.99	**74.93**	73.88	75.96
NeuroNLP2 + single token	48.93	72.29	**78.53**	76.40
NeuroNLP2 + multi token	**63.82**	72.80	77.30	77.59
NeuroNLP2 + NN_g	52.85	72.24	77.02	**78.50**

Table 8: Learning Curve on the DPD dataset. Columns report the number of sentences in the training dataset.

contain tokens that appear less than 10 times helps NN_g to better generalize food names, without focusing on rare and uncommon entities. With this approach the size of the gazetteer is nearly halved, and it is noticeable that 5019 out of 8420 unique tokens in the gazetteer appear only once. Removing common tokens, i.e. those that appear between 10 and 49 times, no model seems to give decent results, with performance lower than the NeuroNLP2 model alone. A last reduction experiment, i.e. removing entities that contain very common tokens, occurring more than 150 times, bringing the gazetteer to a size of only 779 entries, leave NN_g with too few compositions to learn how to generalize, but permits the multi-token approach to give core information to NeuroNLP2, increasing its baseline performance.

	Data Size			
	776 $T_c \geqslant 150$	4366 $T_c \geqslant 50$	12477 $T_c \geqslant 10$	23472 all
NeuroNLP2 + single token	75.90	75.19	70.99	76.40
NeuroNLP2 + multi token	**76.11**	75.05	76.96	77.59
NeuroNLP2 + NN_g	74.63	**75.62**	**79.69**	**78.50**

Table 9: Results of reducing gazetteer size on a *less common* principle; in the columns, the first number is the gazetteer size, while the second element represents the minimum number of occurrences for the tokens in the FOOD gazetteer.

7 Related Work

Although, at least to the best of our knowledge, there is no much work specifically addressing the use of gazetteers in nthe context of neural architectures, still there is a number of related contributions which we discuss in this section.

The use of gazetteers with neural networks has been proposed by (Park et al., 2017), who present a neural network model augmented with syllable embedding vectors, parts-of-speech probability vectors, and gazetteer vectors as input features. Although the proposed model showed good performance, there is no attempt to isolate the impact of gazetteers, which is the goal of our work.

A related approach is presented in (Zhao et al., 2017), which ranked first in English NERC evaluation at KBP 2017. Basically this is an extension of (Lample et al., 2016) that includes entity embedding from gazetteers, where embeddings are derived from a noisy gazetteer created using Wikipedia's articles. The gazetteer is derived from the word-entity statistics from (Park et al., 2017).

A good example of work that builds on the idea of creating a statistical model of named entity starting from gazetteers, is presented in (Al-Olimat et al., 2017). The paper focuses on extracting location names from informal and unstructured texts by identifying referent boundaries. The core of the approach is a statistical language model consisting of a probability distribution over sequences of words (collocations) that represent location names in gazetteers. The algorithm uses the relative likelihood of an observed word sequence to decide the boundaries of a location name in tweets. This is similar in spirit to the NN_g used in our approach, although we make use of a neural model rather than a statistical model.

A second work that it is worth to mention is (Yang et al., 2016), which addresses the problem of using gazetteers when training a neural network with few data. In fact, particularly for massive data scenarios like NER on Twitter, collecting a large amount of high quality gazetteers can alleviate the problem of training data scarcity. The paper shows that large gazetteers may cause a side-effect called 'feature under-training', i.e. gazetteer features overwhelm the training data and may degrade performance. To solve this problem, the authors propose a dropout conditional random fields, which decreases the influence of gazetteer features with a high weight.

8 Conclusions and Future Work

In this paper we were interested to investigate several options about the use of gazetteers in neural architectures for entity recognition. We conducted several experiments on both named entities (CONLL 2003 - English) and nominal entities (food names in DPD - Italian) and showed that: (i) gazetteer features that are extracted by a separately trained the NN_g classifier are more significant than conventional features based on presence-absence of tokens; (ii) integrating such features as extension of the input embedding outperforms integration at the CRF level; (iii) these findings are particularly significant when either the size of the training data or of the gazetteers are reduced.

As a general comment on the use of gazetteers for neural NER, our experiments highlight that gazetteers are much more useful for nominal entities (e.g. food names) than for named entities (e.g. person names). In this respect, the paper shows that the NN_g approach significantly helps to identifying compositional variants of nominal entities.

In the paper we have based our experiments on the neural model described in (Ma and Hovy, 2016). However, very recently, new models (e.g. BERT (Devlin et al., 2018) and ELMO (Peters et al., 2018)) have been proposed, which have further improved performance on Named Entity Recognition. Based on such expectations, we run a preliminary experiment using the multilingual BERT model on the DPD dataset: results, probably due to the poor performance of the model on Italian food, are still significantly lower than NeuroNLP2, and additional work seems to be necessary to properly take advantage of the full capacity of the BERT model.

Finally, as for future work, we intend to apply the current models to a larger number of scenarios, including utterance understanding for conversational agents.

References

Hussein S Al-Olimat, Krishnaprasad Thirunarayan, Valerie Shalin, and Amit Sheth. 2017. Location name extraction from targeted text streams using gazetteer-based statistical language models. *arXiv preprint arXiv:1708.03105*.

Silvana Marianela Bernaola Biggio, Manuela Speranza, and Roberto Zanoli. 2010. Entity mention detection using a combination of redundancy-driven classifiers. In *Proceedings of the Seventh International Conference on Language Resources and Evaluation (LREC'10)*, Valletta, Malta. European Language Resources Association (ELRA).

Jason PC Chiu and Eric Nichols. 2015. Named entity recognition with bidirectional LSTM-CNNs. *arXiv preprint arXiv:1511.08308*.

Jinho D Choi. 2016. Dynamic feature induction: The last gist to the state-of-the-art. In *Proceedings of the 2016 Conference of the North American Chapter of the Association for Computational Linguistics: Human Language Technologies*, pages 271–281.

Jacob Devlin, Ming-Wei Chang, Kenton Lee, and Kristina Toutanova. 2018. Bert: Pre-training of deep bidirectional transformers for language understanding.

George Doddington, Alexis Mitchell, Mark Przybocki, Lance Ramshaw, Stephanie Strassel, and Ralph Weischedel. 2004. The automatic content extraction (ace) program - tasks, data, and evaluation. In *Proceedings of the Fourth International Conference on Language Resources and Evaluation (LREC-2004)*, Lisbon, Portugal. European Language Resources Association (ELRA). ACL Anthology Identifier: L04-1011.

Chris Dyer, Miguel Ballesteros, Wang Ling, Austin Matthews, and Noah A Smith. 2015. Transition-based dependency parsing with stack long short-term memory. *arXiv preprint arXiv:1505.08075*.

Jenny Rose Finkel, Trond Grenager, and Christopher D. Manning. 2005. Incorporating non-local information into information extraction systems by gibbs sampling. In *Proceedings of the 43nd Annual Meeting of the Association for Computational Linguistics (ACL 2005)*, pages 363–370.

Marco Guerini, Simone Magnolini, Vevake Balaraman, and Bernardo Magnini. 2018. Toward zero-shot entity recognition in task-oriented conversational agents. In *Proceedings of the 19th Annual SIGdial Meeting on Discourse and Dialogue*, pages 317–326.

Luheng He, Kenton Lee, Mike Lewis, and Luke Zettlemoyer. 2017. Deep semantic role labeling: What works and whats next. In *Proceedings of the 55th Annual Meeting of the Association for Computational Linguistics (Volume 1: Long Papers)*, volume 1, pages 473–483.

Sepp Hochreiter and Jürgen Schmidhuber. 1997. Long short-term memory. *Neural computation*, 9(8):1735–1780.

John Lafferty, Andrew McCallum, and Fernando CN Pereira. 2001. Conditional random fields: Probabilistic models for segmenting and labeling sequence data.

Guillaume Lample, Miguel Ballesteros, Sandeep Subramanian, Kazuya Kawakami, and Chris Dyer. 2016. Neural architectures for named entity recognition. *CoRR*, abs/1603.01360.

Xuezhe Ma and Eduard Hovy. 2016. End-to-end Sequence Labeling via Bi-directional LSTM-CNNs-CRF. In *Proceedings of the 54th Annual Meeting of the Association for Computational Linguistics (Volume 1: Long Papers)*, volume 1, pages 1064–1074.

Bernardo Magnini, Vevake Balaraman, Mauro Dragoni, Marco Guerini, Simone Magnolini, and Valerio Piccioni. 2018. Ch1: A conversational system to calculate carbohydrates in a meal. In *International Conference of the Italian Association for Artificial Intelligence*, pages 110–122. Springer.

Geonwoo Park, Hyeon-Gu Lee, and Harksoo Kim. 2017. Named entity recognition model based on neural networks using parts of speech probability and gazetteer features. *Advanced Science Letters*, 23(10):9530–9533.

Matthew Peters, Mark Neumann, Mohit Iyyer, Matt Gardner, Christopher Clark, Kenton Lee, and Luke Zettlemoyer. 2018. Deep contextualized word representations. *Proceedings of the 2018 Conference of the North American Chapter of the Association for Computational Linguistics: Human Language Technologies, Volume 1 (Long Papers)*.

Lance A. Ramshaw and Mitchell P. Marcus. 1995. Text chunking using transformation-based learning. *CoRR*, cmp-lg/9505040.

Brian Richards. 1987. Type/token ratios: What do they really tell us? *Journal of child language*, 14(2):201–209.

Erik F Tjong Kim Sang and Fien De Meulder. 2003. Introduction to the conll-2003 shared task: Language-independent named entity recognition. In *Proceedings of the seventh conference on Natural language learning at HLT-NAACL 2003-Volume 4*, pages 142–147. Association for Computational Linguistics.

Eunsuk Yang, Young-Bum Kim, Ruhi Sarikaya, and Yu-Seop Kim. 2016. Drop-out conditional random fields for twitter with huge mined gazetteer. In *Proceedings of the 2016 Conference of the North American Chapter of the Association for Computational Linguistics: Human Language Technologies*, pages 282–288.

Huasha Zhao, Yi Yang, Qiong Zhang, and Luo Si. 2017. Improve neural mention detection and classification via enforced training and inference consistency. *Proc. TAC2017*.

Learning Household Task Knowledge from WikiHow Descriptions

Yilun Zhou
MIT CSAIL
yilun@
mit.edu

Julie A. Shah
MIT CSAIL
julie_a_shah@
csail.mit.edu

Steven Schockaert
Cardiff University
SchockaertS1@
cardiff.ac.uk

Abstract

Commonsense procedural knowledge is important for AI agents and robots that operate in a human environment. While previous attempts at constructing procedural knowledge are mostly rule- and template-based, recent advances in deep learning provide the possibility of acquiring such knowledge directly from natural language sources. As a first step in this direction, we propose a model to learn embeddings for tasks, as well as the individual steps that need to be taken to solve them, based on WikiHow[1] articles. We learn these embeddings such that they are predictive of both step relevance and step ordering. We also experiment with the use of integer programming for inferring consistent global step orderings from noisy pairwise predictions.

1 Introduction

For AI agents to serve as competent (digital or physical) assistants in everyday environments, they need an understanding of the common tasks that people perform. In contrast to factual knowledge, which is encoded to some extent in knowledge graphs such as Freebase (Bollacker et al., 2008), there are currently no resources that capture such knowledge in a comprehensive way.

As a natural solution, in this paper, we consider the problem of learning procedural knowledge from text descriptions, focusing on household tasks as a case study. There are two reasons for this particular focus. First, household tasks require a rich amount of commonsense knowledge, which makes them challenging to deal with for AI agents. Second, learning such knowledge has important applications in the context of household robots and smart home technologies, among others.

The biggest challenge associated with household tasks is the lack of explicit structured information. While specialized datasets for some aspects of household tasks are available (e.g. cooking recipes (Yagcioglu et al., 2018), in-home navigation commands (Matuszek et al., 2013), human action trajectories for chores (Koppula and Saxena, 2013)), general information only exists in natural language format as descriptions intended for human consumption. With recent advances in deep learning and text mining, it is natural to wonder whether, and to what extent, we can acquire knowledge about household tasks from existing textual sources. To start answering this question, in this paper we tap into WikiHow, one of the largest online databases of procedural knowledge. Our aim is to jointly learn two types of knowledge: (i) whether a certain step pertains to a certain task and (ii) how to order two (potentially non-sequential) steps for a given task. We evaluate our learned model both in terms of the performance achieved on these two tasks and by analyzing the resulting embeddings.

2 Related Work

Knowledge Representation A large number of knowledge graphs have already been constructed, capturing a wide variety of human knowledge. These graphs, such as Freebase (Bollacker et al., 2008) and ConceptNet (Liu and Singh, 2004), all share the common structure of using nodes to represent concepts and using edges to represent relations. Among many applications, Williams et al. (2017) showed that ConceptNet can enable better story understanding by capturing some aspects of commonsense knowledge.

However, there is little procedural knowledge in ConceptNet. Instead, planning approaches have traditionally been used to model such knowl-

[1] https://www.wikihow.com

edge. In classical planning languages, such as PDDL (McDermott et al., 1998), the environment is described with a set of predicates and actions are defined in terms of pre-conditions and post-conditions. This turns planning into a search problem. While efficient and provably optimal in small domains, it is hard to model the full spectrum of real world environments with such exact definitions. By contrast, in our work we take a complementary approach, acquiring implicit knowledge from large amounts of data.

Embedding learning Vector space embeddings are commonly used to represent the semantics of linguistic constructs such as words and sentences as vectors in a high-dimensional space. At word level, embedding models such as word2vec (Mikolov et al., 2013) and GloVe (Pennington et al., 2014) are trained based on linguistic context, i.e. the representation of a word depends on the words surrounding mentions of that word in some text corpus. At sentence level, embeddings can be trained from context or learned for one or several downstream applications (Radford et al., 2018; Devlin et al., 2018).

Embeddings for various other kinds of data have also been studied. For example, Chung and Glass (2018) learn vector representations from audio data. Moreover, a large number of methods for embedding graph and network structures have been proposed (Goyal and Ferrara, 2018).

Script knowledge In our work, we learn embeddings for natural language instructions targeted to facilitate commonsense knowledge acquisition. One of the ways in which such embeddings can be used is to rank step instructions for a specific task. Specifically, given the name of the task and two steps, all expressed in natural language, we want our model to predict which step should be done first, using only the embeddings of the task name and steps as input. This problem falls into the general category of learning script knowledge, for which several models have already been proposed. For example, Chambers and Jurafsky (2009) proposed one of the first models to learn script knowledge based on estimated mutual information between events. Modi and Titov (2014) learned embeddings for events such that a linear ranking function operating on embedding space can be used to infer event orders. Pichotta and Mooney (2016a) learned orders from parsed event representation with a LSTM model. Pichotta and Mooney (2016b) used a sentence-level LSTM model that does not require explicit event parsing and extraction.

Knowledge Acquisition from WikiHow There have been many works on collecting knowledge from the web. With specific focus on WikiHow, Chu et al. (2017) used information retrieval and embedding-based clustering to distill a knowledge base of task execution. By using the OpenIE system (Angeli et al., 2015), they inferred relations between tasks and steps so that the distilled knowledge base recognizes that the task in a WikiHow article A is equivalent to a step B in another WikiHow article C, and the user, when reading article C can look up detailed instructions for step B by reading the automatically linked article A. In this way, a hierarchical structure among articles can be extracted.

Park and Motahari Nezhad (2018) used a neural network model to learn specific relations between the steps of each task. Specifically, three relations `is_method_of`, `is_subtask_of`, and `is_alternative_of` are learned using a hierarchical attention neural network that achieved superior performance than standard approaches using an information extraction pipeline.

3 Method

3.1 Dataset Description

We collected a corpus consisting of all WikiHow articles under the category of "Home and Garden[2]", which we believe is most relevant for our purpose of understanding household procedural knowledge. Each WikiHow article describes a particular task, which is composed of a number of steps. Some example tasks are shown in Table 1. Each step is represented by a *gist* and an *explanation*. The gist is a brief and concise summary of the step, such as "purchase packing supplies". The corresponding explanation gives additional contexts and details to the gist. For the previous example, the explanation is as follows:

> "Furniture should generally not be placed in a truck without wrapping it in some sort of protective material. After you've completed your inventory, con-

[2]`https://www.wikihow.com/Category:Home-and-Garden`

Remove Staples with Your Bare Hands
Buy a Shipping Container
Pick Up Broken Glass Splinters
Clean Fireplace Glass
Clean an Espresso Machine

Table 1: A random sample of task titles

Shake your clothes
Move the bowl
Dig a hole about 2 ft deep
Take out the trash
Steam clean older carpets

Table 2: A random sample of task steps

> sider what you'll need to move each piece of furniture..."

Some additional examples of step gists as shown in Table 2.

An additional particularity with WikiHow is that there are two types of article structures. About 30% of all articles have flat structures, which means that an article has a list of individual steps. The remaining ones have 2-level hierarchical structures, which means that an article has several titled subsections, and each subsection has a list of individual steps. For example, an article on "clean kitchen" may include subsections on "organize kitchen shelves", "clean countertop", and "remove oil stain on floor". We found that subsection titles are semantically and syntactically very similar to article titles, so we simply consider each subsection as a separate task. With this preprocessing, the dataset contains 12,431 articles with a total of 162,771 individual steps.[3]

3.2 Model Architecture

A task title t is a list of l natural language words $(w_1, ..., w_l)$. For each word, we use the pre-trained GloVe embedding (Pennington et al., 2014) to look up its vector representation. This embedding is fixed during training. Words which are not in the GloVe vocabulary are represented using a special <unk> token, the embedding for which is learned. We use $\vec{v}_i$ to denote the embedding corresponding to the word w_i. Hence the task title t is represented as $t = (\vec{v}_1, ..., \vec{v}_l)$. The representations for step gists and step explanations are analogous.

[3]The dataset and the model implementation can be downloaded at `https://github.com/YilunZhou/wikihow-embedding/`

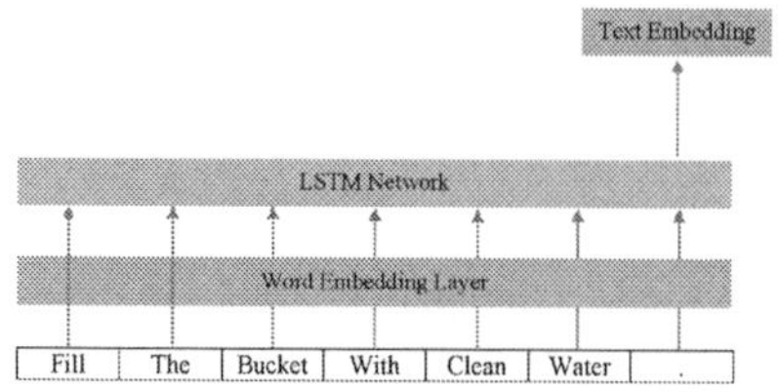

(a) Embedding of task title, step gist, and step explanation

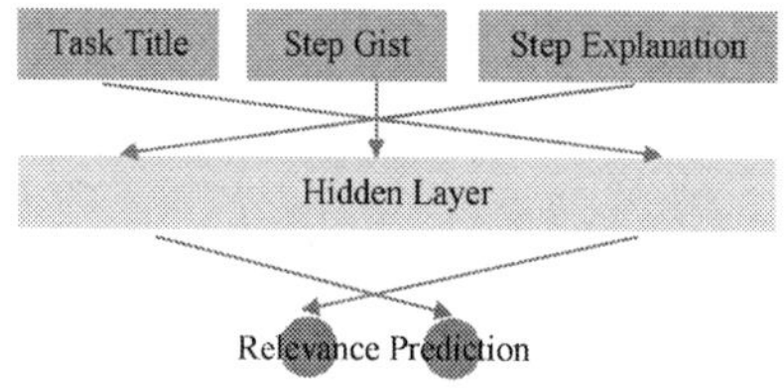

(b) Step relevance prediction

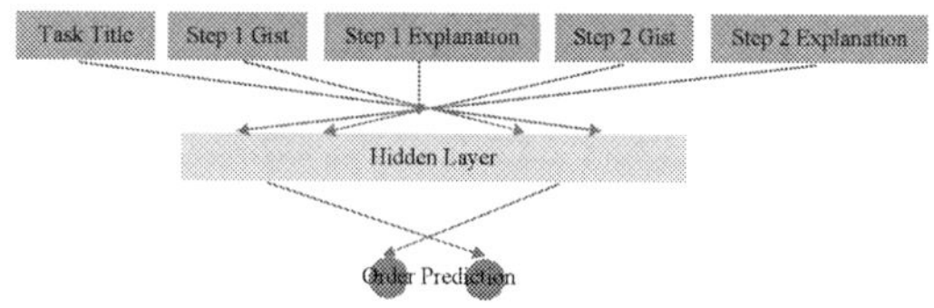

(c) Step order prediction

Figure 1: Model architecture

Figure 1 shows the general workflow of our model. First, three LSTM networks are used to encode the task titles, step gists and step explanations. The input to each of these LSTMs is a list of word vectors, as explained above, and the outputs are the corresponding embeddings, which are taken as the last hidden state of the LSTM encoder. The initial hidden units and memory units of the LSTMs are initialized to 0 (and not updated during training).

3.3 Step Relevance Prediction

Predicting the relevance of a step to a task is a binary classification problem. We first concatenate the embeddings for the task title, step gist, and step explanation together to form the input vector. Then this vector is passed through a hidden layer and an output layer to get the probability that the step is relevant to the task. Negative log-likelihood (NLL) loss is used during training.

3.4 Step Ranking Prediction

Given the task name and two steps from the WikiHow description of that task, we use a similar fully connected network to predict whether a step should happen before another step from the concatenation of embeddings of the task and the two steps, also with NLL loss.

3.5 Joint Prediction of Step Ordering

Given an unordered set of steps, for a given task, the aforementioned neural network can be applied to make a prediction for pairwise step orderings. However, since these predictions are made independently, they may be conflicting with each other (e.g. A is predicted before B, B is predicted before C, and C is predicted before A). Furthermore, we recognize that sometimes two steps can be done in parallel, and a penalty should not be incurred for incorrectly predicting the ordering in which these two steps happen to be ordered in WikiHow. Thus, to be fully flexible with the possibility of "ambiguous" ordering, we employ an integer programming (IP) formulation.

For each pair of steps (i, j), with $i \neq j$, we introduce two binary variables x_{ij} and x_{ji}. The meaning of $x_{ij} = 1$ is that step i has to occur (strictly) before step j, while $x_{ij} = 0$ means that either step i has to occur (strictly) after step j (if $x_{ji} = 1$), or that the ordering does not matter (if $x_{ji} = 0$). Then we set up the following IP problem:

$$
\begin{aligned}
\text{maximize } & \sum_{i,j} w_{ij} x_{ij}, \\
\text{subject to } & x_{ij} \in \{0, 1\} \quad \forall i, j, \\
& x_{ij} + x_{ji} \leq 1 \quad \forall i, j, \\
& x_{ij} + x_{jk} - x_{ik} < 1 \quad \forall i, j, k, \\
& \sum_{i,j} x_{ij} \geq D.
\end{aligned}
$$

In the objective function, we choose $w_{ij} = \log \Pr(i \text{ before } j)$, where this log probability is predicted by the neural network. The first constraint enforces the binary nature of x_{ij}. The second constraint requires that x_{ij} and x_{ji} cannot be both 1, as that would mean that step i is both strictly before and after step j, which is not possible. The third constraint enforces transitivity: if step i is strictly before step j, and step j is also strictly before step k, then we must have that step i is strictly before step k. At this stage, it is easy to see that since $w_{ij} \leq 0$ due to w_{ij} being a log probability, the optimal solution is achieved by choosing $x_{ij} = 0$ for each i and j. Indeed, no penalty is incurred if all pairwise relations are predicted to be ambiguous. For this reason, we have the final constraint which imposes that at least D pairs should be ordered. Note that for a task with T steps, D can be at most $T(T-1)/2$ (i.e. half of all total pairs). Otherwise the second constraint would be unsatisfiable.

3.6 Learning and Inference

We used PyTorch (Paszke et al., 2017) to implement the feed-forward and back-propagation of training, with Adam (Kingma and Ba, 2014) as the optimizer. To solve the integer programming problem, we used CVXPY (Diamond and Boyd, 2016).

4 Experiments

4.1 Data Preparation

We used a 80%/10%/10% split of training, validation, and test data. All reported statistics are from the test set, which is held out during training. Table 3 summarizes the results.

For step relevance prediction tasks, we collected each positive example by sampling a task title and a random step associated with the task. For negative examples, we sampled task titles and steps independently and made sure that the step does not belong to the task. The number of positive and negative examples are balanced.

For step ordering, for each example we sample a task and two steps. Then we randomly denote one of them as step 1 and the other as step 2, and set up the label accordingly.

4.2 Training Details

We used 500-dimensional embeddings throughout, but we found that the learning performance is not sensitive to the embedding dimension, as long as it is over 100. We zero-initialized the hidden and memory cells of the LSTM encoders. The learning rate for the Adam optimizer was set to 0.001.

4.3 Learning Performance

Our model performance is summarized in the first row. In addition, we also tried directly using a bag of word representation as the representation for step explanation, while still keeping the LSTM

	Step relevance	Step ranking
LSTM step explanation	0.911	0.752
bag step explanation	0.902	0.664
no step explanation	0.844	0.657

Table 3: Model performance on two prediction problems

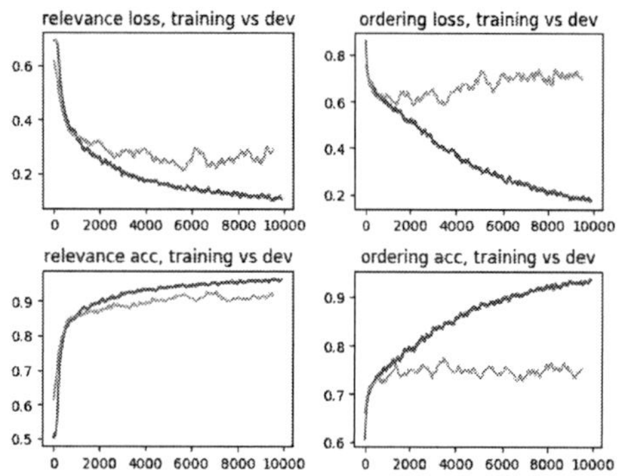

Figure 2: Training/validation loss and accuracy for two tasks

encoder for step gist (second row). Specifically, the embedding of the step explanation is calculated as the average of all embedding vectors for words in the explanation. We also tried not using step explanation information at all, whose performance is shown in the third row.

We see that for both relevance and ranking predictions, the full model with step explanation encoded by an LSTM model performs the best. However, using a bag of words vector representation of step explanations still performs better than not using the step explanation at all, although the improvement is small in the case of step ranking prediction.

The learning curve in Figure 2 shows that while the model is able to get very high accuracy on the training set, the validation accuracy stabilizes after a few thousand iterations, indicating that the model is overfitting to the training set afterwards. The test performance in Table 3 was calculated on the test set using the model iteration that achieves the highest validation accuracy.

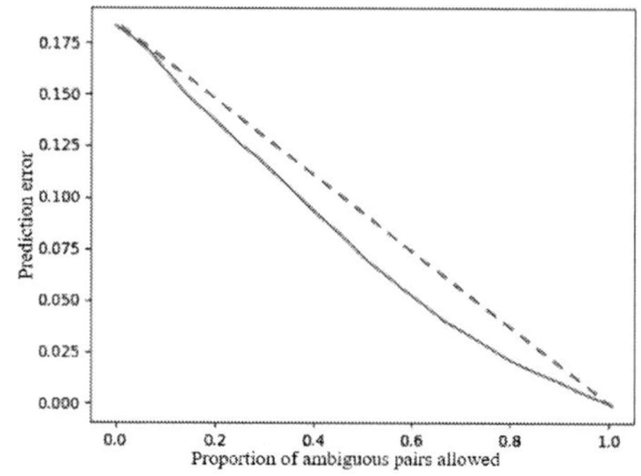

Figure 3: Rank order inference using integer programming

4.4 Integer Programming Inference

In this section, we study if using integer programming inference can provide better ordering performance if we allow the ordering among some pairs to be undecided (i.e. if we set D to be strictly less than half the total number of pairs). Figure 3 presents the result.

The horizontal axis shows the proportion of ambiguous pairs allowed, and the vertical axis shows the proportion of ordering errors. For comparison, we would achieve the red dashed line if we randomly mark pairs as ambiguous, and thus not penalized. We can see that the integer programming inference method is indeed better at identifying ambiguous pairs that, when marked as such, would lead to better performance. However, the improvement is not very substantial, maybe because at training time, the neural network tries to satisfy ambiguous pairs in a way that is more or less arbitrarily defined by the training data, bringing the overall performance down. Thus, one specific idea for future work would be to allow the neural network to intentionally make ambiguous predictions, for which it would not be penalized. Clearly, however, some form of regularization would need to be in place to prevent the network from making the ambiguous prediction too frequently.

4.5 Embedding Visualization

Figure 4 visualizes the embedding of 50 randomly selected tasks, using t-SNE (Maaten and Hinton, 2008) to reduce the dimension to 2. We can see that several clusters of semantically related tasks can be identified, which are indicated by ellipses.

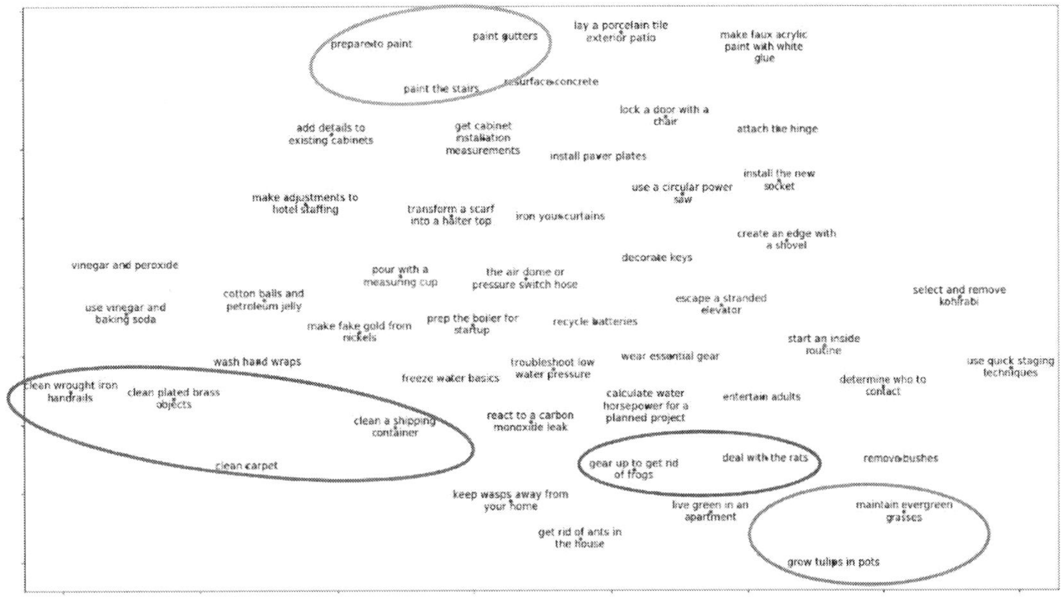

Figure 4: Embedding visualization.

5 Conclusion and Future Work

In this paper, we collected a dataset of natural language instructions for a diverse set of household tasks. We learned a joint embedding of task title and step text for two problems, predicting if a step belongs to a task title and ordering two steps given the task title. We showed that the step relevance can be predicted with a high accuracy if we include the step explanation as part of our model. However, step ordering turned out to be a more challenging problem. We believe that this is at least partly due to noise in the dataset, especially the fact that the ordering of some steps tends to be exchangeable. We also noticed some issues that are specific to WikiHow. For example, the steps which are mentioned for some tasks are more like tips and suggestions.

In terms of future work, one direction is to ground the learned knowledge into some physical systems, such as an in-home robotic platform. Another direction is to try to recognize steps that do not have well-defined orders (Section 4.4), although this is likely to require some additional supervision signal.

6 Acknowledgments

Steven Schockaert has been supported by ERC Starting Grant 637277.

References

Gabor Angeli, Melvin Jose Johnson Premkumar, and Christopher D Manning. 2015. Leveraging linguistic structure for open domain information extraction. In *Proceedings of the 53rd Annual Meeting of the Association for Computational Linguistics and the 7th International Joint Conference on Natural Language Processing (Volume 1: Long Papers)*, volume 1, pages 344–354.

Kurt Bollacker, Colin Evans, Praveen Paritosh, Tim Sturge, and Jamie Taylor. 2008. Freebase: a collaboratively created graph database for structuring human knowledge. In *Proceedings of the 2008 ACM SIGMOD international conference on Management of data*, pages 1247–1250. AcM.

Nathanael Chambers and Dan Jurafsky. 2009. Unsupervised learning of narrative schemas and their participants. In *Proceedings of the Joint Conference of the 47th Annual Meeting of the ACL and the 4th International Joint Conference on Natural Language Processing of the AFNLP: Volume 2-Volume 2*, pages 602–610. Association for Computational Linguistics.

Cuong Xuan Chu, Niket Tandon, and Gerhard Weikum. 2017. Distilling task knowledge from how-to communities. In *Proceedings of the 26th International Conference on World Wide Web*, pages 805–814. International World Wide Web Conferences Steering Committee.

Yu-An Chung and James Glass. 2018. Speech2vec: A sequence-to-sequence framework for learning word embeddings from speech. *arXiv preprint arXiv:1803.08976*.

Jacob Devlin, Ming-Wei Chang, Kenton Lee, and Kristina Toutanova. 2018. Bert: Pre-training of deep bidirectional transformers for language understanding. *arXiv preprint arXiv:1810.04805*.

Steven Diamond and Stephen Boyd. 2016. Cvxpy: A python-embedded modeling language for convex optimization. *The Journal of Machine Learning Research*, 17(1):2909–2913.

Palash Goyal and Emilio Ferrara. 2018. Graph embedding techniques, applications, and performance: A survey. *Knowledge-Based Systems*, 151:78–94.

Diederik P Kingma and Jimmy Ba. 2014. Adam: A method for stochastic optimization. *arXiv preprint arXiv:1412.6980*.

Hema Koppula and Ashutosh Saxena. 2013. Learning spatio-temporal structure from rgb-d videos for human activity detection and anticipation. In *International conference on machine learning*, pages 792–800.

Hugo Liu and Push Singh. 2004. Conceptneta practical commonsense reasoning tool-kit. *BT technology journal*, 22(4):211–226.

Laurens van der Maaten and Geoffrey Hinton. 2008. Visualizing data using t-sne. *Journal of machine learning research*, 9(Nov):2579–2605.

Cynthia Matuszek, Evan Herbst, Luke Zettlemoyer, and Dieter Fox. 2013. Learning to parse natural language commands to a robot control system. In *Experimental Robotics*, pages 403–415. Springer.

Drew McDermott, Malik Ghallab, Adele Howe, Craig Knoblock, Ashwin Ram, Manuela Veloso, Daniel Weld, and David Wilkins. 1998. Pddl-the planning domain definition language.

Tomas Mikolov, Ilya Sutskever, Kai Chen, Greg S Corrado, and Jeff Dean. 2013. Distributed representations of words and phrases and their compositionality. In *Advances in Neural Information Processing Systems (NIPS)*, pages 3111–3119.

Ashutosh Modi and Ivan Titov. 2014. Inducing neural models of script knowledge. In *Proceedings of the Eighteenth Conference on Computational Natural Language Learning*, pages 49–57.

Hogun Park and Hamid Reza Motahari Nezhad. 2018. Learning procedures from text: Codifying how-to procedures in deep neural networks. In *Companion of the The Web Conference 2018 on The Web Conference 2018*, pages 351–358. International World Wide Web Conferences Steering Committee.

Adam Paszke, Sam Gross, Soumith Chintala, Gregory Chanan, Edward Yang, Zachary DeVito, Zeming Lin, Alban Desmaison, Luca Antiga, and Adam Lerer. 2017. Automatic differentiation in pytorch.

Jeffrey Pennington, Richard Socher, and Christopher Manning. 2014. GloVe: Global vectors for word representation. In *Proceedings of the Conference on Empirical Methods in Natural Language Processing (EMNLP)*, pages 1532–1543.

Karl Pichotta and Raymond J Mooney. 2016a. Learning statistical scripts with lstm recurrent neural networks. In *Thirtieth AAAI Conference on Artificial Intelligence*.

Karl Pichotta and Raymond J Mooney. 2016b. Using sentence-level lstm language models for script inference. *arXiv preprint arXiv:1604.02993*.

Alec Radford, Karthik Narasimhan, Tim Salimans, and Ilya Sutskever. 2018. Improving language understanding by generative pre-training.

Bryan Williams, Henry Lieberman, and Patrick H Winston. 2017. Understanding stories with large-scale common sense. In *COMMONSENSE*.

Semih Yagcioglu, Aykut Erdem, Erkut Erdem, and Nazli Ikizler-Cinbis. 2018. Recipeqa: A challenge dataset for multimodal comprehension of cooking recipes. *arXiv preprint arXiv:1809.00812*.

A Sequence Modeling Approach for Structured Data Extraction from Unstructured Text

Jayati Deshmukh*
IIIT-Bangalore
jayati.deshmukh@iiitb.org

Annervaz KM
Accenture Technology Labs
annervaz.k.m@accenture.com

Shubhashis Sengupta
Accenture Technology Labs
shubhashis.sengupta@accenture.com

Abstract

Extraction of structured information from unstructured text has always been a problem of interest for NLP community. Structured data is concise to store, search and retrieve; and it facilitates easier human & machine consumption. Traditionally, structured data extraction from text has been done by using various parsing methodologies, applying domain specific rules and heuristics. In this work, we leverage the developments in the space of sequence modeling for the problem of structured data extraction. Initially, we posed the problem as a machine translation problem and used the state-of-the-art machine translation model. Based on these initial results, we changed the approach to a sequence tagging one. We propose an extension of one of the attractive models for sequence tagging tailored and effective to our problem. This gave 4.4% improvement over the vanilla sequence tagging model. We also propose another variant of the sequence tagging model which can handle multiple labels of words. Experiments have been performed on Wikipedia Infobox Dataset of biographies and results are presented for both single and multi-label models. These models indicate an effective alternate deep learning technique based methods to extract structured data from raw text.

1 Introduction

A humongous volume of data in the form of text, images, audio and video is being generated daily. It has been reported that 90% of all the data available today has been generated in the last two years (DoMo, 2017). The pace of data generation is growing exponentially. The generation of data is not only restricted to open domains and social media; even in closed groups like private organizations and corporations, textual data is being produced in abundance. Unstructured data is present in a variety of forms like documents, reports and surveys, logs etc. Restricting this data to be captured directly in structured form prohibits the natural capturing of the data, leaving out essential pieces. But structured data presents the data in a concise and well-defined manner which is easier to understand than a corresponding document. Structured data can be transformed into tables which can be easily stored in databases. It can be indexed, queried for and searched to retrieve relevant results of a query. Thus structured representation is quintessential to facilitate machine consumption of data. Moreover in the world of data abundance, such structured representation is essential for human consumption as well.

In many business processes, like Finance and Healthcare, the transformation of the unstructured data into structured form is done manually or semi-automatically through domain specific rules and heuristics. Let's take the example of *Pharmacovigilance* (Maitra et al., 2014), where adverse effects of prescribed drugs are reported by patients or medical practitioners. This information is used to detect signals of adverse effects. Collection, analysis and reporting of these adverse effects by the drug companies is mandated by law. In most cases, it is easy for patients or medical practitioners to describe the side-effects of their drugs in a common, day to day language, in free form text. Then it has to be transformed into a structured format which is analyzed with clinical knowledge for signals of adverse effects. Currently this is done by human analysts or through very rigid text processing heuristics for certain kinds of text. Another domain is extraction and management of legal contracts in domains such as real estate. Specifically *Lease Abstraction* involves manual inspection and validation of commercial rental lease documents. It is done by offshore experts who extract relevant information

*Work done at Accenture Technology Labs

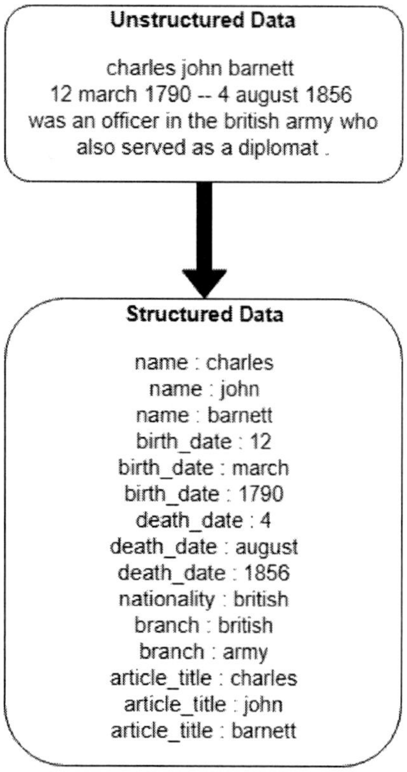

Figure 1: From Unstructured to Structured Data

from the documents into a structured form. This structured information is further used for aggregate analytics and decision making by large real estate firms (Annervaz et al., 2015).

Figure 1 shows a sample unstructured text and its corresponding structured output. In case the structured data is to be stored in a database, the labels like *name*, *birth_date* etc can be the column names of the database and the corresponding values like *charles* and *12 march 1970* can be the actual values stored.

As mentioned earlier, previous work in this space involved parsing the natural language sentences, and writing rules and heuristics on the parse tree or structure to extract the information required (Culotta and Sorensen, 2004; Fundel et al., 2006; Reichartz et al., 2009). In this work, we approach the problem from sequence modeling perspective and weave together state of the art models in the space to extract structured information from raw unstructured data. The task of information extraction to build structured data can be described as generating or matching appropriate tags or labels to corresponding parts of raw data. For each token in the raw data, a corresponding tag is attached marking what kind of data it stands for. *OTHER* tag gets attached if the data in the raw text is not relevant.

We have approached the problem both from machine translation and sequence tagging perspectives. In machine translation, typically there are two sequences, one in source language (say English) and the other in target language (say French). Machine learning models try to convert the sequence of tokens in source language to sequence of tokens in target language. In case of translation problem, the core idea being expressed in the input and the output is the same, however it is in a different language. Similarly, for our problem both the input and output have same content although it is represented in an unstructured or structured format. So to start with, we approach the problem from translation perspective and treat the source text as word sequence of unstructured text and the corresponding tag sequence as target sequence. State of the art machine translation models (sequence to sequence model (Cho et al., 2014; Sutskever et al., 2014)) can then be attempted for the same. We have experimented with this approach and treat it as our baseline. We didn't find any previous work on this dataset for structured data extraction task. However we realized that this problem cannot be directly mapped to a translation problem. There is significantly more word or phrase level information in the input which cannot be appropriately represented by translation models. We realized that sequence tagging models (like for POS tagging (Huang et al., 2015)) are more suitable for this problem. We have experimented with state of the art sequence tagging model for the problem and propose some problem specific variants to improve the performance.

Main contributions of this work are as follows:

1. We approach the problem from sequence modeling perspective, which is perhaps the first attempt in literature to the best of our knowledge. Modeled this way, we can eliminate usage of traditional ways for parsing or writing domain specific rules. A parallel corpus of unstructured and structured data is sufficient to train the models.

2. We have designed a modified version of the state of the art sequence tagging model along with PoS tags and attention which further im-

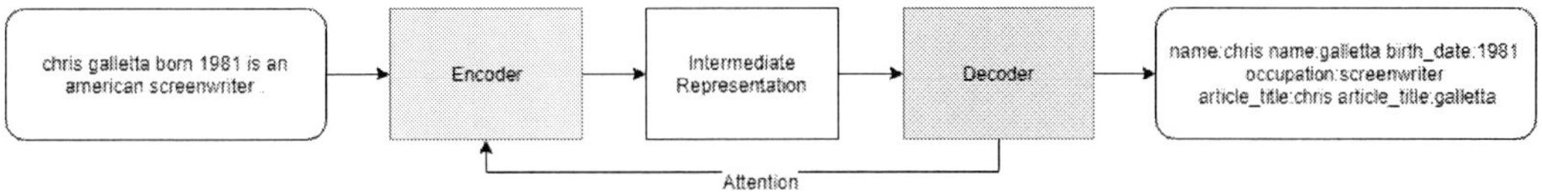

Figure 2: Seq2seq Example

proves the results compared to the vanilla sequence tagging model.

3. We have also designed a multi-label sequence tagging model which can generate multiple labels of words using a customized learning loss based on Set similarity.

The paper is organized as follows: We present the details of seq2seq and sequence tagging models in Section 2 along with some interesting work which has been done previously using these models. In Section 3 we give details of our approach along with details of vanilla model and modified models for single and multi-label problems. The details of our experiments are in Section 4. We present some related work in Section 5. We conclude in Section 6 by giving some future work directions.

2 Preliminaries

A variety of NLP problems have been solved using both seq2seq models and sequence tagging models. These models and their variants have produced state-of-the-art results and we discuss these models and some of their applications in the following subsection.

2.1 Seq2Seq Models

Seq2seq models are end to end models which transform an input sequence into an output sequence. These models basically consist of an encoder which takes the input and encodes it into an intermediate representation and a decoder which takes the intermediate representation as input and generates the output sequence, one token at a time. Encoders and Decoders structurally may be Recurrent Neural Networks like RNN, LSTM, GRU (Cho et al., 2014; Sutskever et al., 2014)) or even Convolutional Neural Networks (Gehring et al., 2017), depending on the problem it is designed to solve. It might also have different variations and additional features like attention, multiple layers etc (Bahdanau et al., 2014). These were the first citizens of *Encode, Attend, Decode* paradigm deep learning models.

Seq2seq models generate output in two steps as shown in Figure 2. Firstly x, the sequence of embeddings which is created by combining the embeddings (vectors) of words, is given as input to the encoder. The encoder transforms x into an intermediate representation z (which for example for RNN encoder may be the hidden state at the end of processing input) as follows

$$z = enc(x)$$

Next, this representation is given as input to the decoder. It generates the output Y token by token as $w_0, w_1, w_2, ..., w_l$ from z as per the following equations:

$$h_t = dec(h_{t-1}, w_t)$$

$$s_t = g(h_t)$$

$$p_t = softmax(s_t)$$

where, at $t = 1$

$$h_0 = z$$

$$w_0 = w_{sos}$$

Here, at $t = 1$, h_0 is the output of encoder z and w_0 is the embedding of *start of sentence* tag. The decoder takes the previous hidden state and current word embedding as input to generate the next hidden state. Next, function g transforms the hidden representation from hidden dimension h to the dimension of vocabulary v. Next its output is passed through a softmax function which transforms the input into probability values for each word in the vocabulary. Finally, it is passed through argmax function to fetch the index of the word of maximum probability and returns the corresponding word. This process is repeated till *end of sentence* tag is generated by the decoder.

Originally, seq2seq models were conceived for language translation task(Cho et al., 2014; Sutskever et al., 2014)), where the input text is in one language like English and the output which is its translation, is in another language like French.

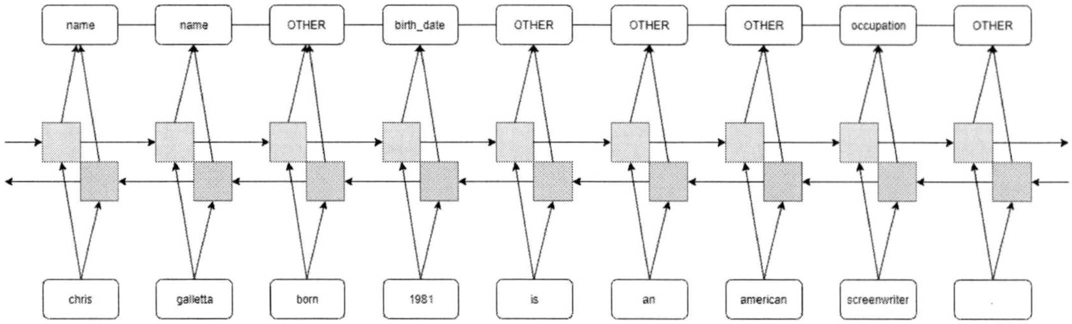

Figure 3: Sequence Tagging Example

These simple models generated encouraging results leading to production grade models which parallelize training on multiple GPUs and are used in applications such as Google Translate (Wu et al., 2016). Seq2seq models have also been used for Text Summarization. In this case, the input is a large document and output is its summary which can be used for generating news headlines or abstracts. For this purpose, an attention based encoder and a beam search decoder which generated words from the vocabulary gave the best results (Rush et al., 2015; Wu et al., 2016).

Seq2seq models are not just restricted to textual input/outputs. There have been applications with image inputs to automatically generate captions of images using CNN encoder and RNN decoder with attention (Vinyals et al., 2015). These models have also been used on speech data to transform speech to text (Chorowski et al., 2015). They have also been used with videos for video translation, subtext generation and video generation etc (Venugopalan et al., 2014; Srivastava et al., 2015; Yao et al., 2015). Some multi-modal models which take more that one forms of inputs have also been successful (Kiros et al., 2014).

2.2 Sequence Tagging Models

Sequence tagging or labeling models tag all the tokens in the input sequence. Fundamentally, this model consists of recurrent neural network like RNN, LSTM, GRU and Convolutional Neural Network which reads input at token level and a conditional random field (CRF) (Lafferty et al., 2001) which takes as input the encoded representation and generates corresponding tags for each token. These models may also include other additional features like word and sentence features, regularization, attention etc. Originally this model was conceived for tasks like Part of Speech (PoS) tagging, chunking and Named Entity Recognition (NER) (Huang et al., 2015). A joint model for multiple tasks also seems to work well (Hashimoto et al., 2016).

A high level representation of sequence tagging model as shown is Figure 3. Here the input is passed into an bi-LSTM and the hidden vector $h(t)$ and output vector $y(t)$ are generated as follows:

$$h_f(t) = f(U_f x(t) + W_f h_f(t-1))$$

$$h_b(t) = f(U_b x(t) + W_b h_b(t-1))$$

$$h(t) = [h_f(t) : h_b(t)]$$

$$y(t) = g(Vh(t))$$

where $h_f(t)$ and $h_b(t)$ are the hidden representations of the forward and backward LSTMs respectively. These two are concatenated to generate the final hidden representation $h(t)$. U_f, W_f, U_b, W_b, V are weights computed during training. These bi-LSTM representations are combined with CRF using Viterbi Decoder (Sutton et al., 2012). It takes the hidden state and the previously generated tags in the form of sequence to generate the next tag. If the string of output tags is taken as a sequence, then we can say that the CRF generates the most likely sequence out of all possible output sequences (Huang et al., 2015; Ma and Hovy, 2016; Lample et al., 2016)

3 Approach and Models

For our problem, we started with seq2seq models. We then moved to vanilla sequence tagging models which we realized are more suitable for the task as compared to seq2seq models. We also built a variant of sequence tagging model suitable for our problem which further improves the performance.

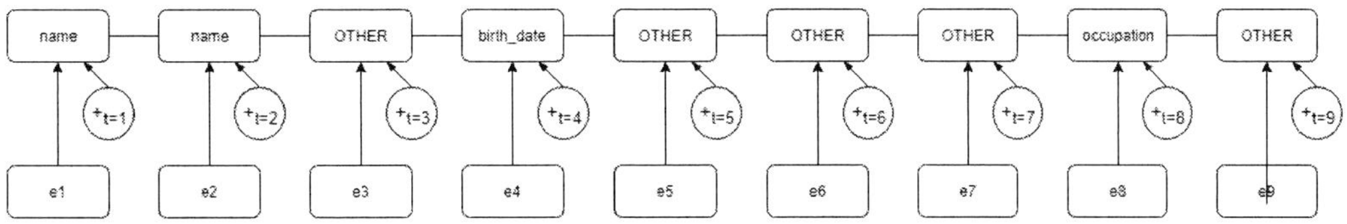

Figure 4: Sequence Tagging with Attention

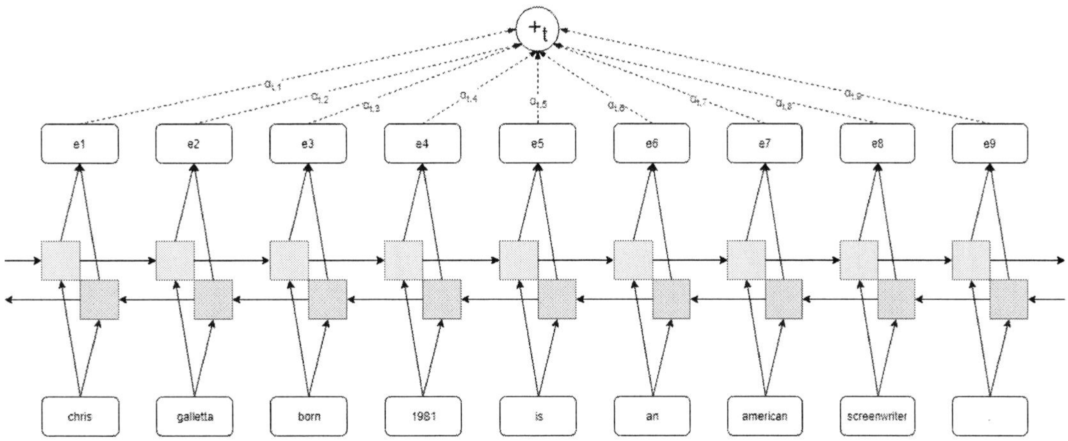

Figure 5: Computing Attention

Finally, a sequence tagging model which can generate multiple labels for each token has also been designed. Further details of the models are presented in the following subsections.

3.1 Baseline Approach : Seq2seq model

For seq2seq model, the input is the sentence or set of sentences and the structured output is transformed to a string which is a series of key-value pairs corresponding to the word-label pairs of the sentence. Here we assume that the tags are at a word level. This model can learn multiple labels of the same word for example *chris* is *name* as well as *article_title* in Figure 2. This model by its design also learns the sequence of label-word pairs. Experiments as detailed in Section 4 have been performed on different combinations of RNN and CNN encoders and decoders.

3.2 Vanilla Sequence Tagging model

Sequence tagging model reads the input word by word and simultaneously generates the corresponding label for the word as shown in Figure 3. Here, blue cells represent the forward LSTM and the violet cells represent the backward LSTM. The line between the output labels represents the CRF. For this model, the data is transformed such that the sentence is split in words by spaces and then each word is tagged to a corresponding label. Only the first label of a word is considered. If a word does not have any label then it is manually labeled as 'OTHER'. Structurally this biLSTM-CRF model can comparatively work better even in case of longer inputs. However, this model cannot learn multiple labels of a word. The model generates labels at a word level and thus it does not have an ordering as in case of seq2seq models.

3.3 Modified Sequence Tagging model

We have modified the vanilla sequence tagging model to incorporate following variations which models our problem better and was found to generate improved results. Part of Speech (PoS) tags of words carry rich information and are connected to the corresponding labels of each word. To utilize this, we used the word itself and the PoS tag of each word as input. We randomly initialized the PoS tag embeddings. Word embeddings and PoS tag embeddings were concatenated and passed as input to the bi-LSTM. We believe that while generating label for the current word, not all the words of the input are equally important. Words nearby to the current word are contextually more important compared to words farther away. Thus, every word has different importance or weight while generating the label of cur-

Table 1: Sample Results

Table 2: Single Label Results

Sentence 1	Label 1	Sentence 2	Label 2
w.	name	renan	name
lamont	name	luce	name
was	OTHER	born	OTHER
a	OTHER	5	birth_date
scottish	OTHER	march	birth_date
footballer	OTHER	1980	birth_date
who	OTHER	,	birth_place
played	OTHER	paris	birth_place
as	OTHER	is	OTHER
a	OTHER	a	OTHER
right	position	french	OTHER
winger	position	singer	occupation
.	OTHER	and	OTHER
		songwriter	occupation
		.	OTHER

Table 3: Multi-Label Results

Word	Labels
begziin	article_title name
yavuukhulan	article_title image name
,	OTHER
1929-1982	OTHER
was	OTHER
a	OTHER
mongolian	nationality language
poet	occupation
of	OTHER
the	OTHER
communist	OTHER
era	OTHER
that	OTHER
wrote	OTHER
in	caption
mongolian	nationality language
and	OTHER
russian	language
.	OTHER

rent word. To incorporate this in the model, we used self-attention (Vaswani et al., 2017; Tan et al., 2018) as depicted in Figure 4 and 5.

3.4 Multi-label Sequence Tagging model

As shown in Figure 1 a word can have multiple associated tags / labels. Vanilla sequence tagging models are designed to predict only a single tag for each word. Thus a lot of information might be lost by using these models. The following modified model can give multiple possible labels of words. At the output layer, instead of using softmax which was used in single label prediction case, we use sigmoid which normalizes each of the label prediction scores between 0 and 1 independently. We used hamming loss, which is the most common metric used in case of multi-label classification problems (Tsoumakas and Vlahavas, 2007; Elisseeff and Weston, 2002). Hamming loss is defined as the fraction of wrong labels to total number of labels. It takes into account both correct and incorrect labels. Let y_t be the vector of true labels and y_p be the vector of independent probabilities of predicted labels. Then Hamming Loss (HL) is computed as follows:

$$HL = y_t \; XOR \; y_p$$

Here, XOR is non-differentiable and cannot be used to train the multi-label sequence tagging model. To overcome this problem, the HL equation is transformed as below:

$$HL_{diff} = average(y_t * (1 - y_p) + (1 - y_t) * y_p)$$

For example, let a word have true labels as $[1, 0, 0, 1]$ and the model predicts the labels $[0.9, 0.1, 0.2, 0.9]$, then hamming loss in this case is computed as $avg([1, 0, 0, 1] * [0.1, 0.9, 0.8, 0.1] + [0, 1, 1, 0] * [0.9, 0.1, 0.2, 0.9])$ or $avg(0.1 + 0.1 + 0.1 + 0.2)$ or 0.125.

4 Experiments & Results

We have used the Wikipedia Infobox dataset created by (Lebret et al., 2016) which is available in the public domain[1]. It consists of total $728,321$ biographies, each having the first Wikipedia paragraph and the corresponding infobox, both of which have been tokenized. Originally this dataset

[1] https://github.com/DavidGrangier/wikipedia-biography-dataset

Table 4: Baseline Results - Seq2Seq Model

Model	Accuracy %	Perplexity
CNN Encoder Decoder	63.34	5.78
LSTM Encoder Decoder	68.42	3.95
LSTM Encoder Decoder with PoS	69.60	3.45

Table 5: Sequence Tagging Results

Model	Accuracy %	F1 Score %
biLSTM-CRF	79.34	65.00
biLSTM-CRF with PoS & Attention	82.82	62.32

was created to build models to generate text based on the the infobox. In our case, the problem is reversed. Given a paragraph of unstructured data, we try to generate the corresponding infobox or structured data. In the dataset, some information might be present in the paragraph but not in infobox and vice versa. We have pruned the infoboxes so that it contains only that information which is present in the paragraph. The information which is not present in the paragraph cannot be generated by any model by itself without external knowledge.

We have split the dataset into three parts in the ratio 8:1:1 for train, validation and test. We have done basic pre-processing on both paragraphs and infoboxes. Extra information and labels tagged as none have been removed from infoboxes. The words have been initialized to GloVe (Pennington et al., 2014) embeddings and character embeddings (Santos and Zadrozny, 2014) have been randomly initialized. Words are 300 dimensional and characters are 100 dimensional. The models have been trained for 15 epochs or until it showed no improvement. Single label model has been trained using Adam Optimizer (Kingma and Ba, 2014) and multi-label model using Adagrad Optimizer (Zou and Shen, 2018). Adaptive learning rate has been used. Dropouts (Guo et al., 2016) have been used as regularizer. Table 1 shows some sample results of single and multi-label sequence tagging models.

Table 4 shows the Accuracy and Perplexity scores of the baseline approach using seq2seq model. Here, accuracy is calculated as total number of correctly predicted words by total number of words. Perplexity metric is from NLP models and it represents probability distribution of a language model over the text[2]. Lower perplexity represents better generalization and thus better performance. We observed that LSTM Encoder-Decoder performs better than CNN Encoder-Decoder as it is able to take the temporal order or words into account and also because it handles short / medium length text well. We also gave sequence of words and corresponding PoS tags as input and the results of this were the best among all the seq2seq models. Despite these enhancements, this model does not perform well and has a low accuracy.

Table 5 shows the Sequence Tagging results on the same data using vanilla model and other model variants described earlier. In this case, accuracy metric is computed as number of labels correctly predicted by total number of words and F1 score is calculated as usual as the harmonic mean of precision and recall. We present the results of vanilla model and sequence tagging model with improvements like PoS tags and attention. We notice that the results of sequence tagging models are significantly better than the seq2seq models. In multi-label sequence tagging model, the hamming loss on the test dataset was 0.1927.

5 Related Work

Traditionally relationships have been extracted from raw text using dependency parse tree based methods (Culotta and Sorensen, 2004; Reichartz et al., 2009). Dependency parse tree shows the grammatical dependency among the words or phrases of the input sentence. To extract relation among words from a dependency parse tree, classifiers are trained to classify the relation. Sometimes rules are applied on on dependency parse

[2] http://www.cs.virginia.edu/~kc2wc/teaching/NLP16/slides/04-LMeval.pdf

trees to further improve the results (Fundel et al., 2006; Atzmueller et al., 2008). These rule based models have shown improved results and have been used in medical domain. It might also fare well in closed domain areas where there is less variation in text. Even at a Web scale, there have been efforts to extract information specifically in the form of named entities and relationships using DBpedia spotlight (Mendes et al., 2011) and OpenIE (Pasca et al., 2006). A joint entity and relation extraction model (Miwa and Bansal, 2016) is primarily built using LSTMs. It comprises two LSTM models - word sequence LSTM predicts the entities and dependency tree LSTM predicts the relationships among the entities. They also use additional features like PoS tags, dependency types etc as input. However in our models, we label the words of raw text, these labels are not categorized into entities and relationships. The datasets on which they have performed the experiments contain very few (< 10) entities and relations as compared to our labels (1000). Attention based encoder-decoder model (Dong and Lapata, 2016) has been used to convert raw text to logical format. The output is not entity or relationship but a logical string corresponding to the input. They show that this model gives consistent results across different domains and logical formats. The seq2seq model which we used as a baseline is similar to this model.

6 Conclusion & Future Work

We proposed a deep learning based approach for the age old NLP problem of information extraction. We have used multiple variants of deep learning based sequence tagging models to extract structured data from unstructured data. Large publicly available dataset of Wikipedia Biographies has been used in experiments to prove the efficacy. Sequence tagging models further improved with additional features like PoS tags and attention mechanism. Multi-label sequence tagging model gave more complete results from practical perspective. Unlike the traditional methods, our models are generic and not dependent on the structure of Wikipedia Infobox dataset. Similarly, it is also not dependent on English language specifically. Ideally, it should work well for other similar languages or datasets. A parallel corpus of unstructured data and its corresponding structured data is all that is required to train these models. The actual performance might be affected by language specific issues like word order, double negation or other grammatical issues. And there might be minor modifications needed specific for different datasets or languages.

To the best of our knowledge, this is the first attempt in using sequence models for structured data extraction. Being an initial work, there are plethora of possible future work extensions. In the practical setting, the information to be extracted tends to be hierarchical. So the tags have a hierarchical structure to it. Current model proposed, handles only flat tag structure. Alterations to incorporate and handle hierarchical tag structure is one direction of work we are considering. In the Wikipedia Infobox dataset the text from where the structured information is extracted is already identified or don't have large span. In practice, this is not the case. The text usually have larger span, this makes the problem tougher. We have to devise models first to prioritize the text snippets from where the information has to be extracted, such an end-to-end trainable model is another direction of work. Similarly there are lot of options for future work, we hope our initial work and results will inspire the community to work in these directions.

References

K. M. Annervaz, Jovin George, and Shubhashis Sengupta. 2015. A generic platform to automate legal knowledge work process using machine learning. In *14th IEEE International Conference on Machine Learning and Applications, ICMLA 2015*, pages 396–401.

Martin Atzmueller, Peter Kluegl, and Frank Puppe. 2008. Rule-based information extraction for structured data acquisition using textmarker. In *LWA*, pages 1–7.

Dzmitry Bahdanau, Kyunghyun Cho, and Yoshua Bengio. 2014. Neural machine translation by jointly learning to align and translate. *arXiv preprint arXiv:1409.0473*.

Kyunghyun Cho, Bart Van Merriënboer, Caglar Gulcehre, Dzmitry Bahdanau, Fethi Bougares, Holger Schwenk, and Yoshua Bengio. 2014. Learning phrase representations using rnn encoder-decoder for statistical machine translation. *arXiv preprint arXiv:1406.1078*.

Jan K Chorowski, Dzmitry Bahdanau, Dmitriy Serdyuk, Kyunghyun Cho, and Yoshua Bengio. 2015. Attention-based models for speech recognition. In *Advances in neural information processing systems*, pages 577–585.

Aron Culotta and Jeffrey Sorensen. 2004. Dependency tree kernels for relation extraction. In *Proceedings of the 42nd annual meeting on association for computational linguistics*, page 423. Association for Computational Linguistics.

DoMo. 2017. *Data Never Sleeps 5.0.*

Li Dong and Mirella Lapata. 2016. Language to logical form with neural attention. *arXiv preprint arXiv:1601.01280.*

André Elisseeff and Jason Weston. 2002. A kernel method for multi-labelled classification. In *Advances in neural information processing systems*, pages 681–687.

Katrin Fundel, Robert Küffner, and Ralf Zimmer. 2006. Relexrelation extraction using dependency parse trees. *Bioinformatics*, 23(3):365–371.

Jonas Gehring, Michael Auli, David Grangier, Denis Yarats, and Yann N Dauphin. 2017. Convolutional sequence to sequence learning. *arXiv preprint arXiv:1705.03122.*

Yanming Guo, Yu Liu, Ard Oerlemans, Songyang Lao, Song Wu, and Michael S Lew. 2016. Deep learning for visual understanding: A review. *Neurocomputing*, 187:27–48.

Kazuma Hashimoto, Caiming Xiong, Yoshimasa Tsuruoka, and Richard Socher. 2016. A joint many-task model: Growing a neural network for multiple nlp tasks. *arXiv preprint arXiv:1611.01587.*

Zhiheng Huang, Wei Xu, and Kai Yu. 2015. Bidirectional lstm-crf models for sequence tagging. *arXiv preprint arXiv:1508.01991.*

Diederik P Kingma and Jimmy Ba. 2014. Adam: A method for stochastic optimization. *arXiv preprint arXiv:1412.6980.*

Ryan Kiros, Ruslan Salakhutdinov, and Richard S Zemel. 2014. Unifying visual-semantic embeddings with multimodal neural language models. *arXiv preprint arXiv:1411.2539.*

John Lafferty, Andrew McCallum, and Fernando CN Pereira. 2001. Conditional random fields: Probabilistic models for segmenting and labeling sequence data.

Guillaume Lample, Miguel Ballesteros, Sandeep Subramanian, Kazuya Kawakami, and Chris Dyer. 2016. Neural architectures for named entity recognition. *arXiv preprint arXiv:1603.01360.*

Rémi Lebret, David Grangier, and Michael Auli. 2016. Neural text generation from structured data with application to the biography domain. *arXiv preprint arXiv:1603.07771.*

Xuezhe Ma and Eduard Hovy. 2016. End-to-end sequence labeling via bi-directional lstm-cnns-crf. *arXiv preprint arXiv:1603.01354.*

Anutosh Maitra, K. M. Annervaz, Tom Geo Jain, Madhura Shivaram, and Shubhashis Sengupta. 2014. A novel text analysis platform for pharmacovigilance of clinical drugs. In *Proceedings of the Complex Adaptive Systems 2014 Conference - Conquering Complexity: Challenges and Opportunities*, pages 322–327.

Pablo N Mendes, Max Jakob, Andrés García-Silva, and Christian Bizer. 2011. Dbpedia spotlight: shedding light on the web of documents. In *Proceedings of the 7th international conference on semantic systems*, pages 1–8. ACM.

Makoto Miwa and Mohit Bansal. 2016. End-to-end relation extraction using lstms on sequences and tree structures. *arXiv preprint arXiv:1601.00770.*

Marius Pasca, Dekang Lin, Jeffrey Bigham, Andrei Lifchits, and Alpa Jain. 2006. Organizing and searching the world wide web of facts-step one: the one-million fact extraction challenge. In *AAAI*, volume 6, pages 1400–1405.

Jeffrey Pennington, Richard Socher, and Christopher Manning. 2014. Glove: Global vectors for word representation. In *Proceedings of the 2014 conference on empirical methods in natural language processing (EMNLP)*, pages 1532–1543.

Frank Reichartz, Hannes Korte, and Gerhard Paass. 2009. Dependency tree kernels for relation extraction from natural language text. In *Joint European Conference on Machine Learning and Knowledge Discovery in Databases*, pages 270–285. Springer.

Alexander M Rush, Sumit Chopra, and Jason Weston. 2015. A neural attention model for abstractive sentence summarization. *arXiv preprint arXiv:1509.00685.*

Cicero D Santos and Bianca Zadrozny. 2014. Learning character-level representations for part-of-speech tagging. In *Proceedings of the 31st International Conference on Machine Learning (ICML-14)*, pages 1818–1826.

Nitish Srivastava, Elman Mansimov, and Ruslan Salakhudinov. 2015. Unsupervised learning of video representations using lstms. In *International conference on machine learning*, pages 843–852.

Ilya Sutskever, Oriol Vinyals, and Quoc V Le. 2014. Sequence to sequence learning with neural networks. In *Advances in neural information processing systems*, pages 3104–3112.

Charles Sutton, Andrew McCallum, et al. 2012. An introduction to conditional random fields. *Foundations and Trends® in Machine Learning*, 4(4):267–373.

Zhixing Tan, Mingxuan Wang, Jun Xie, Yidong Chen, and Xiaodong Shi. 2018. Deep semantic role labeling with self-attention. In *Thirty-Second AAAI Conference on Artificial Intelligence.*

Grigorios Tsoumakas and Ioannis Vlahavas. 2007. Random k-labelsets: An ensemble method for multilabel classification. In *European conference on machine learning*, pages 406–417. Springer.

Ashish Vaswani, Noam Shazeer, Niki Parmar, Jakob Uszkoreit, Llion Jones, Aidan N Gomez, Łukasz Kaiser, and Illia Polosukhin. 2017. Attention is all you need. In *Advances in neural information processing systems*, pages 5998–6008.

Subhashini Venugopalan, Huijuan Xu, Jeff Donahue, Marcus Rohrbach, Raymond Mooney, and Kate Saenko. 2014. Translating videos to natural language using deep recurrent neural networks. *arXiv preprint arXiv:1412.4729.*

Oriol Vinyals, Alexander Toshev, Samy Bengio, and Dumitru Erhan. 2015. Show and tell: A neural image caption generator. In *Computer Vision and Pattern Recognition (CVPR), 2015 IEEE Conference on*, pages 3156–3164. IEEE.

Yonghui Wu, Mike Schuster, Zhifeng Chen, Quoc V Le, Mohammad Norouzi, Wolfgang Macherey, Maxim Krikun, Yuan Cao, Qin Gao, Klaus Macherey, et al. 2016. Google's neural machine translation system: Bridging the gap between human and machine translation. *arXiv preprint arXiv:1609.08144.*

Li Yao, Atousa Torabi, Kyunghyun Cho, Nicolas Ballas, Christopher Pal, Hugo Larochelle, and Aaron Courville. 2015. Describing videos by exploiting temporal structure. In *Proceedings of the IEEE international conference on computer vision*, pages 4507–4515.

Fangyu Zou and Li Shen. 2018. On the convergence of adagrad with momentum for training deep neural networks. *arXiv preprint arXiv:1808.03408.*

LIAAD at SemDeep-5 Challenge: Word-in-Context (WiC)

Daniel Loureiro, Alípio Mário Jorge
LIAAD - INESC TEC
Faculty of Sciences - University of Porto, Portugal
dloureiro@fc.up.pt, amjorge@fc.up.pt

Abstract

This paper describes the LIAAD system that was ranked second place in the Word-in-Context challenge (WiC) featured in SemDeep-5. Our solution is based on a novel system for Word Sense Disambiguation (WSD) using contextual embeddings and full-inventory sense embeddings. We adapt this WSD system, in a straightforward manner, for the present task of detecting whether the same sense occurs in a pair of sentences. Additionally, we show that our solution is able to achieve competitive performance even without using the provided training or development sets, mitigating potential concerns related to task overfitting.

1 Task Overview

The Word-in-Context (WiC) (Pilehvar and Camacho-Collados, 2019) task aims to evaluate the ability of word embedding models to accurately represent context-sensitive words. In particular, it focuses on polysemous words which have been hard to represent as embeddings due to the meaning conflation deficiency (Camacho-Collados and Pilehvar, 2018). The task's objective is to detect if target words occurring in a pair of sentences carry the same meaning.

Recently, contextual word embeddings from ELMo (Peters et al., 2018) or BERT (Devlin et al., 2019) have emerged as the successors to traditional embeddings. With this development, word embeddings have become context-sensitive by design and thus more suitable for representing polysemous words. However, as shown by the experiments of (Pilehvar and Camacho-Collados, 2019), they are still insufficient by themselves to reliably detect meaning shifts.

In this work, we propose a system designed for the larger task of Word Sense Disambiguation (WSD), where words are matched with specific senses, that can detect meaning shifts without being trained explicitly to do so. Our WSD system uses contextual word embeddings to produce sense embeddings, and has full-coverage of all senses present in WordNet 3.0 (Fellbaum, 1998). In Loureiro and Jorge (2019) we provide more details about this WSD system, called LMMS (Language Modelling Makes Sense), and demonstrate that it's currently state-of-the-art for WSD. For this challenge, we employ LMMS in two straightforward approaches: checking if the disambiguated senses are equal, and training a classifier based on the embedding similarities. Both approaches perform competitively, with the latter taking the second position in the challenge ranking, and the former trailing close behind even though it's tested directly on the challenge, forgoing the training and development sets.

2 System Description

LMMS has two useful properties: 1) uses contextual word embeddings to produce sense embeddings, and 2) covers a large set of over 117K senses from WordNet 3.0. The first property allows for comparing precomputed sense embeddings against contextual word embeddings generated at test-time (using the same language model). The second property makes the comparisons more meaningful by having a large selection of senses at disposal for comparison.

2.1 Sense Embeddings

Given the meaning conflation deficiency issue with traditional word embeddings, several works have focused on adapting Neural Language Models (NLMs) to produce word embeddings that are more sense-specific. In this work, we start producing sense embeddings from the approach used by recent works in contextual word embeddings, particularly context2vec (Melamud et al., 2016) and

ELMo (Peters et al., 2018), and introduce some improvements towards full-coverage and more accurate representations.

2.1.1 Using Supervision

Our set of full-coverage WordNet sense embeddings is bootstrapped from the SemCor corpus (Miller et al., 1994). Sentences containing sense-annotated tokens (or spans) are processed by a NLM in order to obtain contextual embeddings for those tokens. After collecting all sense-labeled contextual embeddings, each sense embedding ($\vec{v}_s$) is determined by averaging its corresponding contextual embeddings. Formally, given n contextual embeddings $\vec{c}$ for some sense s:

$$\vec{v}_s = \frac{1}{n} \sum_{i=1}^{n} \vec{c}_i$$

In this work, we used BERT as our NLM. For replicability, these are the relevant details: 1024 embedding dimensions, 340M parameters, cased. Embeddings result from the sum of top 4 layers ([-1, -4]). Moreover, since BERT uses WordPiece tokenization that doesn't always map to token-level annotations, we use the average of subtoken embeddings as the token-level embedding.

2.1.2 Extending Supervision

Despite its age, SemCor is still the largest sense-annotated corpus. The lack of larger sets of sense annotations is a major limitation of supervised approaches for WSD (Le et al., 2018). We address this issue by taking advantage of the semantic relations in WordNet to extend the annotated signal to other senses. Missing sense embeddings are inferred (i.e. imputed) from the aggregation of sense embeddings at different levels of abstraction from WordNet's ontology. Thus, a synset embedding corresponds to the average of all of its sense embeddings, a hypernym embedding corresponds to the average of all of its synset embeddings, and a lexname embedding corresponds to the average of a larger set of synset embeddings. All lower abstraction representations are created before next-level abstractions to ensure that higher abstractions make use of lower-level generalizations. More formally, given all missing senses in WordNet $\hat{s} \in W$, their synset-specific sense embeddings $S_{\hat{s}}$, hypernym-specific synset embeddings $H_{\hat{s}}$, and lexname-specific synset embeddings $L_{\hat{s}}$, the procedure has the following stages:

$$(1) \quad if|S_{\hat{s}}| > 0, \qquad \vec{v}_{\hat{s}} = \tfrac{1}{|S_{\hat{s}}|} \textstyle\sum \vec{v}_s, \forall \vec{v}_s \in S_{\hat{s}}$$

$$(2) \quad if|H_{\hat{s}}| > 0, \quad \vec{v}_{\hat{s}} = \tfrac{1}{|H_{\hat{s}}|} \textstyle\sum \vec{v}_{syn}, \forall \vec{v}_{syn} \in H_{\hat{s}}$$

$$(3) \quad if|L_{\hat{s}}| > 0, \quad \vec{v}_{\hat{s}} = \tfrac{1}{|L_{\hat{s}}|} \textstyle\sum \vec{v}_{syn}, \forall \vec{v}_{syn} \in L_{\hat{s}}$$

2.1.3 Leveraging Glosses

There's a long tradition of using glosses for WSD, perhaps starting with the popular work of Lesk (1986). As a sequence of words, the information contained in glosses can be easily represented in semantic spaces through approaches used for generating sentence embeddings. While there are many methods for generating sentence embeddings, it's been shown that a simple weighted average of word embeddings performs well (Arora et al., 2017).

Our contextual embeddings are produced from NLMs that employ attention mechanisms, assigning more importance to some tokens over others. As such, these embeddings already come 'pre-weighted' and we embed glosses simply as the average of all of their contextual embeddings (without preprocessing). We've found that introducing synset lemmas alongside the words in the gloss helps induce better contextualized embeddings (specially when glosses are short). Finally, we make our dictionary embeddings ($\vec{v}_d$) sense-specific, rather than synset-specific, by repeating the lemma that's specific to the sense alongside all of the synset's lemmas and gloss words. The result is a sense-level embedding that is represented in the same space as the embeddings we described in the previous section, and can be trivially combined through concatenation (previously L_2 normalized).

Given that both representations are based on the same NLM, we can make predictions for contextual embeddings of target words w (again, using the same NLM) at test-time by simply duplicating those embeddings, aligning contextual features against sense and dictionary features when computing cosine similarity. Thus, we have sense embeddings $\vec{v}_s$, to be matched against duplicated contextual embeddings $\vec{c}_w$, represented as follows:

$$\vec{v}_s = \begin{bmatrix} ||\vec{v}_s||_2 \\ ||\vec{v}_d||_2 \end{bmatrix}, \vec{c}_w = \begin{bmatrix} ||\vec{c}_w||_2 \\ ||\vec{c}_w||_2 \end{bmatrix}$$

2.2 Sense Disambiguation

Having produced our set of full-coverage sense embeddings, we perform WSD using a simple Nearest-Neighbors (k-NN) approach, similarly to Melamud et al. (2016) and Peters et al. (2018). We match the contextual word embedding of a target word against the sense embeddings that share the word's lemma (see Figure 1). Matching is performed using cosine similarity (with duplicated features on the contextual embedding for alignment, as explained in 2.1.3), and the top match is used as the disambiguated sense.

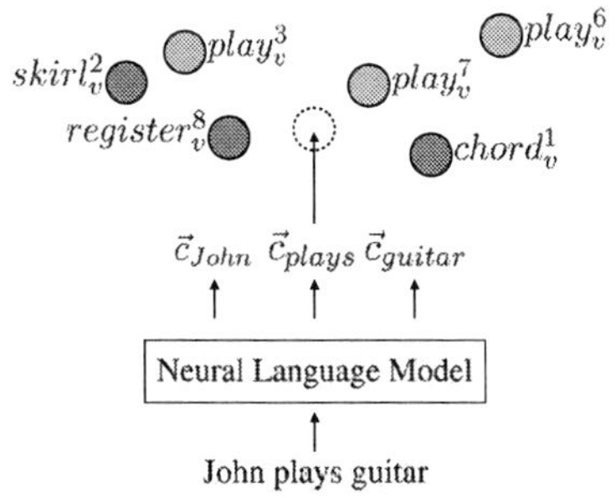

Figure 1: Illustration of our k-NN approach for WSD, which relies on full-coverage sense embeddings represented in the same space as contextualized embeddings.

2.3 Binary Classification

The WiC task calls for a binary judgement on whether the meaning of a target word occurring in a pair of sentences is the same or not. As such, our most immediate solution is to perform WSD and base our decision on the resulting senses. This approach performs competitively, but we've still found it worthwhile to use WiC's data to train a classifier based on the strengths of similarities between contextual and sense embeddings. In this section we explore the details of both approaches.

2.3.1 Sense Comparison

Our first approach is a straightforward comparison of the disambiguated senses assigned to the target word in each sentence. Considering the example in Figure 2, this approach simply requires checking if the sense $cook_v^2$ assigned to 'makes' in the first sentence equals the sense $produce_v^2$ assigned to the same word in the second sentence.

2.3.2 Classifying Similarities

The WSD procedure we describe in this paper represents sense embeddings in the same space as contextual word embeddings. Our second approach exploits this property by considering the similarities (including between different embedding types) that can be seen in Figure 2. In this approach, we take advantage of WiC's training set to learn a Logistic Regression Binary Classifier based on different sets of similarities. The choice of Logistic Regression is due to its explainability and lightweight training, besides competitive performance. We use sklearn's implementation (v0.20.1), with default parameters.

3 Results

The best system we submitted during the evaluation period of the challenge was a Logistic Regression classifier trained on two similarity features (sim_1 and sim_2, or contextual and sense-level). We obtained slightly better results with a classifier trained on all four similarities shown in Figure 2, but were unable to submit that system due to the limit of a maximum of three submissions during evaluation. Interestingly, the simple approach described in 2.3.1 achieved a competitive performance of 66.3 accuracy, without being trained or fine tuned on WiC's data. Performance of best entries and baselines can be seen on Table 1.

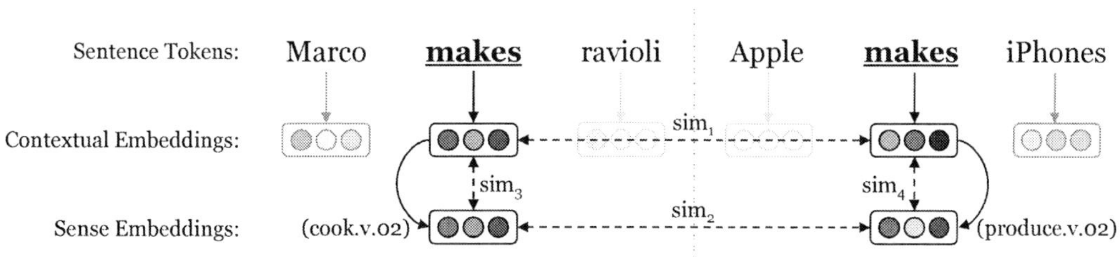

Figure 2: Components and interactions involved in our approaches. The sim_n labels correspond to cosine similarities between the related embeddings. Sense embeddings obtained from 1-NN matches of contextual embeddings.

Submission	Acc.
SuperGlue (Wang et al., 2019)	68.36
LMMS (Ours)	67.71
Ensemble (Soler et al., 2019)	66.71
ELMo-weighted (Ansell et al., 2019)	61.21
BERT-large	65.5
Context2vec	59.3
ELMo-3	56.5
Random	50.0

Table 1: Challenge results at the end of the evaluation period. Bottom results correspond to baselines.

4 Analysis

In this section we provide additional insights regarding our best approach. In Table 2, we show how task performance varies with the similarities considered.

Model	sim_n	Dev	Test
M0	N/A	68.18	66.29
M1	1	67.08	64.64
M2	2	66.93	66.21
M3	1, 2	68.50	67.71
M4	1, 2, 3, 4	69.12	**68.07**

Table 2: Accuracy of our different models. M0 wasn't trained on WiC data, the other models were trained on different sets of similarites. We submitted M3, but achieved slightly improved results with M4.

We determined that our best system (M4, using four features) obtains a precision of 0.65, recall of 0.82, and F1 of 0.73 on the development set, showing a relatively high proportion of false positives (21.6% vs. 9.25% of false negatives). This skewness can also be seen in the probability distribution chart at Figure 3. Additionally, we also present a ROC curve for this system at Figure 4 for a more detailed analysis of the system's performance.

5 Conclusion and Future Work

We've found that the WiC task can be adequately solved by systems trained for the larger task of WSD, specially if they're based on contextual embeddings, and when compared to the reported baselines. Still, we've found that the WiC dataset can be useful to learn a classifier that builds on top of the WSD system for improved performance on WiC's task of detecting shifts in meaning. In future work, we believe this improved ability to detect shifts in meaning can also assist WSD, particularly in generating semi-supervised datasets. We share our code and data at github.com/danlou/lmms.

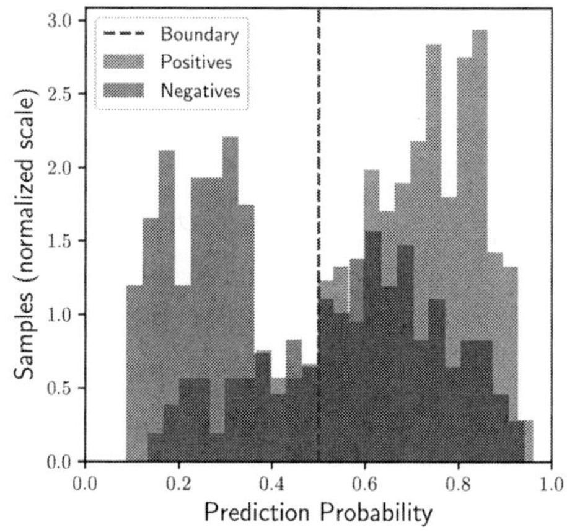

Figure 3: Distribution of Prediction Probabilities across labels, as evaluated by our best model on the development set.

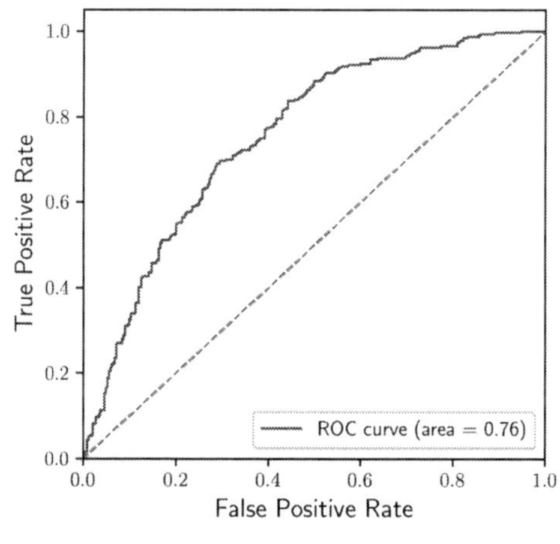

Figure 4: ROC curve for results of our best model on the development set.

Acknowledgements

This work is financed by National Funds through the Portuguese funding agency, FCT - Fundação para a Ciência e a Tecnologia within project: UID/EEA/50014/2019.

References

Alan Ansell, Felipe Bravo-Marquez, and Bernhard Pfahringer. 2019. An elmo-inspired approach to semdeep-5's word-in-context task. In *SemDeep-5@IJCAI 2019*, page forthcoming.

Sanjeev Arora, Yingyu Liang, and Tengyu Ma. 2017. A simple but tough-to-beat baseline for sentence embeddings. In *International Conference on Learning Representations (ICLR)*.

Jose Camacho-Collados and Mohammad Taher Pilehvar. 2018. From word to sense embeddings: A survey on vector representations of meaning. *J. Artif. Int. Res.*, 63(1):743–788.

Jacob Devlin, Ming-Wei Chang, Kenton Lee, and Kristina Toutanova. 2019. BERT: Pre-training of deep bidirectional transformers for language understanding. In *Proceedings of the 2019 Conference of the North American Chapter of the Association for Computational Linguistics: Human Language Technologies, Volume 1 (Long and Short Papers)*, pages 4171–4186, Minneapolis, Minnesota. Association for Computational Linguistics.

Christiane Fellbaum. 1998. In *WordNet : an electronic lexical database*. MIT Press.

Minh Le, Marten Postma, Jacopo Urbani, and Piek Vossen. 2018. A deep dive into word sense disambiguation with LSTM. In *Proceedings of the 27th International Conference on Computational Linguistics*, pages 354–365, Santa Fe, New Mexico, USA. Association for Computational Linguistics.

Michael Lesk. 1986. Automatic sense disambiguation using machine readable dictionaries: How to tell a pine cone from an ice cream cone. In *Proceedings of the 5th Annual International Conference on Systems Documentation*, SIGDOC '86, pages 24–26, New York, NY, USA. ACM.

Daniel Loureiro and Alípio Jorge. 2019. Language modelling makes sense: Propagating representations through wordnet for full-coverage word sense disambiguation. In *Proceedings of the 57th Annual Meeting of the Association for Computational Linguistics*, page forthcoming, Florence, Italy. Association for Computational Linguistics.

Oren Melamud, Jacob Goldberger, and Ido Dagan. 2016. context2vec: Learning generic context embedding with bidirectional LSTM. In *Proceedings of The 20th SIGNLL Conference on Computational Natural Language Learning*, pages 51–61, Berlin, Germany. Association for Computational Linguistics.

George A. Miller, Martin Chodorow, Shari Landes, Claudia Leacock, and Robert G. Thomas. 1994. Using a semantic concordance for sense identification. In *HUMAN LANGUAGE TECHNOLOGY: Proceedings of a Workshop held at Plainsboro, New Jersey, March 8-11, 1994.*

Matthew Peters, Mark Neumann, Mohit Iyyer, Matt Gardner, Christopher Clark, Kenton Lee, and Luke Zettlemoyer. 2018. Deep contextualized word representations. In *Proceedings of the 2018 Conference of the North American Chapter of the Association for Computational Linguistics: Human Language Technologies, Volume 1 (Long Papers)*, pages 2227–2237, New Orleans, Louisiana. Association for Computational Linguistics.

Mohammad Taher Pilehvar and Jose Camacho-Collados. 2019. Wic: the word-in-context dataset for evaluating context-sensitive meaning representations. In *Proceedings of NAACL*, Minneapolis, United States.

Aina Garí Soler, Marianna Apidianaki, and Alexandre Allauzen. 2019. Limsi-multisem at the ijcai semdeep-5 wic challenge: Context representations for word usage similarity estimation. In *SemDeep-5@IJCAI 2019*, page forthcoming.

Alex Wang, Yada Pruksachatkun, Nikita Nangia, Amanpreet Singh, Julian Michael, Felix Hill, Omer Levy, and Samuel R. Bowman. 2019. Superglue: A stickier benchmark for general-purpose language understanding systems. *CoRR*, abs/1905.00537.

LIMSI-MultiSem at the IJCAI SemDeep-5 WiC Challenge: Context Representations for Word Usage Similarity Estimation

Aina Garí Soler[1], Marianna Apidianaki[1,2] and Alexandre Allauzen[1]

[1]LIMSI, CNRS, Univ. Paris Sud, Université Paris-Saclay, F-91405 Orsay, France
[2]LLF, CNRS, Univ. Paris-Diderot
{aina.gari,marianna,allauzen}@limsi.fr

Abstract

We present the LIMSI-MultiSem system submitted to the IJCAI-19 SemDeep-5 WiC challenge. The system measures word usage similarity in sentence pairs. We experiment with cosine similarities of word and sentence embeddings of different types, and with features based on in-context substitute annotations automatically assigned to WiC sentence pairs. The model with the highest performance on the WiC development set uses a combination of cosine similarities from different embedding types. It obtains an accuracy of 66.7 on the shared task test set and is ranked third among the participating systems.

1 Introduction

The SemDeep-5 WiC shared task proposes to identify the intended meaning of words in context. It is framed as a binary classification task that addresses whether two instances of a target word have the same meaning (Pilehvar and Camacho-Collados, 2019). The WiC dataset contains 7,466 sentence pairs and is proposed as a new evaluation benchmark for context-sensitive word representations.

We apply to this task the method from Garí Soler et al. (2019) which addresses the usage similarity of contextualized instances of words. The method integrates cosine similarities from different types of context-sensitive embeddings and in-context automatic substitutes. Our best system combines cosine similarities from three embedding types. It obtains an accuracy of 66.7 on the WiC test set, and is ranked third among all systems that participated in the task.

2 The WiC Dataset

The WiC dataset contains 7,466 sentence pairs of target words automatically labelled as having the same (T) or different (F) meaning. It was automatically compiled by extracting usage examples and sense information from lexical resources (WordNet (Fellbaum, 1998) VerbNet (Schuler, 2006) and Wiktionary[1]). To exclude instance pairs describing fine-grained sense distinctions, the resource was automatically pruned based on synset proximity in the WordNet network. Human accuracy upper bound on the dataset was defined as 80%, which corresponds to the average human accuracy on a sample of sentence pairs (Pilehvar and Camacho-Collados, 2019). Inter-annotator agreement was at the same level. The WiC dataset provides a benchmark for evaluating context-sensitive word representations, and their capacity to capture the dynamic aspects of word meaning and usage.

3 Contextualized Representations

Our proposed model computes a contextualized representation for each target word instance in a WiC sentence pair using different types of embeddings. The cosine similarity of the obtained vector representations is used as a feature for our classifier. We use the following types of embeddings:

SIF (Smooth Inverse Frequency): Simple method for deriving sentence representations from uncontextualized embeddings (Arora et al., 2017). Dimensionality reduction is applied to a weighted average of the vectors of words in a sentence. Weighting is based on word frequency in Common Crawl. We use SIF in combination with 300-*d* GloVe vectors trained on Common Crawl (Pennington et al., 2014).[2]

Context2vec: Neural model that learns embeddings for words and their contexts simultaneously (Melamud et al., 2016). It is based on word2vec's

[1]http://www.wiktionary.org/
[2]https://nlp.stanford.edu/projects/glove/

CBOW (Mikolov et al., 2013), but replaces the averaging of context word embeddings with a biLSTM that learns a representation of a sentence excluding the target word. We use a 600-*d* model pre-trained on the UkWac corpus (Baroni et al., 2009).[3]

ELMo (Embeddings from Language Models): Contextualized word representations obtained from the internal states of a deep bidirectional LSTM trained with a language model objective (Peters et al., 2018). Instead of learning the best linear combination of layer representations for a task – a common way of using ELMo – we use out-of-the-box 512-*d* embeddings.[4] We experiment with the top layer, and the average of the three hidden layers. We represent each WiC sentence in two ways: a) with the ELMo embedding corresponding to the target word, and b) with the average of ELMo embeddings of all words in the sentence. We also average the embeddings at a context window of size two, as this was shown to work better for word usage similarity with ELMo (Garí Soler et al., 2019).

BERT (Bidirectional Encoder Representations from Transformers): Representations obtained from a 12-layer bidirectional Transformer encoder trained with a language model objective where words on both sides of the target word in a sentence are masked and need to be predicted (Devlin et al., 2018). The pre-trained BERT architecture can be fine-tuned for specific tasks, but its internal contextualized word representations can also be used directly, similar to ELMo. We use 768-*d* uncased BERT representations of the target word, and the average of all words in a sentence.

USE (Universal Sentence Encoder): General-purpose sentence encoder trained with multi-task learning (Cer et al., 2018). Using transfer learning, USE improves performance on different NLP tasks at the sentence and phrase level (e.g. sentiment analysis). We use the Deep Averaging Network (DAN) encoder,[5] where input word and bigram embeddings are averaged and fed through a feedforward neural network, to create embeddings for WiC sentences.

[3] `http://u.cs.biu.ac.il/~nlp/resources/downloads/context2vec/`

[4] The medium-sized model at `https://allennlp.org/elmo`.

[5] `https://tfhub.dev/google/universal-sentence-encoder/2`

4 Automatic Substitution

Manual substitute annotations have been useful for in-context usage similarity estimation (Erk et al., 2009; McCarthy et al., 2016). The idea is that a high proportion of shared substitutes between two word instances reflects their semantic similarity.[6]

Extending previous work where manual substitute annotations were used to estimate usage similarity (Erk et al., 2009), we automatically annotate WiC instances with substitutes, and use features based on their overlap for our classifier. We use the context2vec method for automatic lexical substitution (Melamud et al., 2016). Given a sentence with a new instance of a target word t, and a set of candidate substitutes for the word ($S = s_1, s_2, ..., s_n$), context2vec ranks all candidates taking into account the target-to-substitute similarity and the substitute-to-context similarity.

$$c2v\_score = \frac{cos(s,t)+1}{2} \times \frac{cos(s,C)+1}{2} \quad (1)$$

In Formula 1, s and t are the context2vec word embeddings of a candidate substitute and the target, and C is the context vector of the sentence. The pool of candidate substitutes for a target word is formed from its set of paraphrases in the Paraphrase Database (PPDB) XXL package (Ganitkevitch et al., 2013; Pavlick et al., 2015).[7]

For every instance, context2vec ranks all candidates available for the target. Therefore, the generated ranking (R) always contains the same substitutes, in the same or different order. To make substitute overlap measures (McCarthy et al., 2016) operational in this setting, we use a filtering strategy from Garí Soler et al. (2019). The method detects a cut-off point in the ranking R that reflects a shift from good quality substitutes (high-ranked), to substitutes that are not a good fit in the context (low-ranked). It checks whether adjacent substitutes are paraphrases in PPDB; if not, it discards everything found after that point in R.

After filtering the ranking R for each sentence pair, we obtain three different features based on the retained substitutes.

- **Common substitutes:** The proportion of shared substitutes between the two instances of a target word.

[6] Previous work explores graded usage similarity, whereas in WiC it is binary.

[7] `http://paraphrase.org/`

Target	Sentences	Substitutes
way	Do you know the **way** to the airport?	ways, route, path, road {*connection, means, journey, move, direction, gateway, passage, place, ...*}
	He said he was looking for the **way** out.	ways, path, road, route, walk {*day, right, passage, move, means, time, doorway, ...*}
drink	Can I buy you a **drink**?	beer {*bottle, beverage, pint, vodka, booze, whisky, wine, liquor, drunk, cocktail, restaurant, ...*}
	He took a **drink** of his beer and smacked his lips.	swig {*bottle, pint, sip, drinking, beverage, drank, beer, drunk, cup, booze, liquor, ...*}

Table 1: Sentence pairs from the WiC training set for the noun *way* (gold label: T) and the verb *drink* (gold label: F) with automatic substitute annotations assigned by context2vec. Substitutes in italics were discarded after filtering.

- **GAP score:** GAP (Generalized Average Precision) considers the order of ranked elements and their weights (Kishida, 2005). GAP score ranges from 0 to 1 (for perfect disagreement/agreement). We take the average score between the rankings produced for a sentence pair in both directions ($GAP(R_1, R_2)$ and $GAP(R_2, R_1)$). Weights are the scores assigned to the substitutes by context2vec. We use the GAP implementation shared by Melamud et al. (2015).

- **Substitute cosine similarity**. We form pairs of substitutes from R_1 and R_2, and calculate the average of their GloVe cosine similarities. This feature accounts for the semantic similarity of substitutes, which can also, to some extent, reflect usage similarity.

A few WiC sentence pairs (5%) contain target words that are not present in the PPDB XXL package.[8] We apply automatic substitution to instances of target words that have paraphrases in PPDB, and back off to a classifier that uses only embedding-based features for the rest.[9] Table 1 shows examples of WiC sentences with automatic substitutes, before and after filtering.

5 Training Data Augmentation

We extend the WiC training data with 4,018 sentence pairs automatically extracted from the Concepts in Context (CoInCo) corpus (Kremer et al., 2014). CoInCo is a subset of the MASC corpus (Ide et al., 2008) which contains manual substitute annotations for all content words in a sentence. We use a balanced collection of similar (T) and dissimilar (F) sentence pairs from CoInCo, with labels automatically assigned based on substitute overlap (Garí Soler et al., 2019).[10] We apply the automatic substitution method described in Section 4, and extract substitute- and embedding-based features to be used by our models.

6 Model Development

We train a logistic regression classifier on the WiC training set, and experiment with different feature combinations on the development set. We use cosine similarities of different embedding representations. For ELMo and BERT, we try several layer combinations,[11] the target word vector and the sentence vector (see Section 3). For ELMo, we also apply a context window of size 2. The best configuration for BERT is the average of the last four layers, and for ELMo, the context window approach. We then combine the best embedding features for prediction. We also train models with the substitute-based features only, backing off to the best embedding-based model for instances of words not present in PPDB. We combine the best embedding- and substitute-based features in the Combined setting.

We apply the BERT and ELMO configurations that gave best results on the WiC development set to the setting with additional CoInCo data (WiC+CnC), and repeat the experiments. Results on the WiC development set are given in Table 2. Substitute-based features do not help the model,

[8]For full coverage, an option would be to use the whole vocabulary as a pool, as in the original context2vec implementation.

[9]PPDB paraphrases were available for target words in 97% of training, 89% of development and 90% of test sentence pairs in WiC.

[10]https://github.com/ainagari/coinco_usim_data/

[11]The average of the three layers or the top layer for ELMo. The top layer, the second-to-last layer, the average and the concatenation of the last four layers for BERT.

Features	WiC	WiC+CnC
BERT avg 4 tw	66.46	65.99
USE	63.64	63.48
ELMo top cw=2	62.38	61.76
SIF	60.66	59.56
c2v	60.34	61.13
BERT, USE	67.87	68.03
BERT, USE, ELMo	**68.65**	68.18
BERT, USE, ELMo, SIF	68.03	-
BERT, USE, ELMo, c2v	-	**68.34**
Substitute-based	60.34	57.84
Combined	66.77	68.34

Table 2: Accuracy of the models with embedding-based and substitute features on the WiC development set. We report results of the models trained only on WiC, and on the extended (WiC+CnC) dataset. The best configurations (marked in boldface) were applied to the WiC test set.

probably because of the noise in automatic annotations. The best result is obtained by the model trained only on WiC that uses cosine similarities from BERT, USE and ELMo. In the WiC+CnC setting, the Combined model gets the same performance as the model that uses four embedding types (BERT, USE, ELMo and c2v). We apply the simpler embedding-based model to the WiC test set.

7 Results and Analysis

Results of the two best-performing models (in boldface in Table 2) on the WiC test set are given in Table 3. Our best model is the one trained only on WiC, which uses BERT, USE and ELMo cosine similarities. It was ranked third at the competition with an accuracy of 66.71, which is higher than all results reported in the WiC description paper (Pilehvar and Camacho-Collados, 2019).

The additional training data extracted from CoInCo does not help the models. We believe this to be due to the different kind of sense distinctions present in the dataset extracted from CoInCo and in WiC. To explore this hypothesis, we take a closer look at the model predictions and carry out a qualitative analysis of the sense distinctions in the two datasets. The confusion matrices of the two best models on the development set show that wrong predictions most often concern dissimilar (*F*) sentence pairs. This type of error occurs more with the model trained on WiC+CnC (67% of total errors compared to 59% when training only on

Approach	Accuracy
WiC BERT, USE, ELMo	66.71
WiC+CnC BERT, USE, ELMo, c2v	65.64
BERT_{large} Threshold (Pilehvar and Camacho-Collados, 2019)	63.8

Table 3: Accuracy of our two best models on the WiC test set, compared to the best result from previous work.

WiC). A quick observation of WiC data reveals that dissimilar (*F*) pairs sometimes describe related senses, in spite of the pruning that aimed at excluding these from the dataset (Pilehvar and Camacho-Collados, 2019).

We extract a random sample of 60 sentence pairs from the CoInCo training data and the WiC development set to explore whether they differ in this respect. We manually annotate all pairs for graded usage similarity, using a scale of 1 (completely different) to 5 (the same), as in Erk et al. (2009). Our assumption is that *F* pairs that describe related senses will be assigned higher similarity scores. A comparison of the graded usage similarity values of gold *F* instances reveals that these values differ significantly in CoInCo and WiC ($p = 0.048$), as determined by a Mann-Whitney test, with WiC *F* pairs having a higher average similarity score (3.19 ± 1.52) than CoInCo *F* pairs (2.53 ± 0.19). The following *F* sentence pair from WiC is an example where the target word (*construction*) expresses different but closely related meanings (as a process and a result): *Construction is underway on the new bridge – The engineer marvelled at his construction*. The CoInCo sentence pairs extracted by Garí Soler et al. (2019) that we use for training describe more clear-cut sense distinctions, due to the process used for their extraction, based on the overlap of manually annotated substitutes (see Section 5).

8 Conclusion and Future Work

We propose a new model for word usage similarity estimation. The LIMSI-MULTISEM system combines different types of context-sensitive word and sentence representations with features derived from automatic substitution for usage similarity prediction. The best configuration combines cosine similarities from three embedding types: BERT, USE and ELMo.

In future work, we plan to use our model to investigate usage similarity on a per lemma basis, in order to identify lemmas with clear-cut and fuzzy sense distinctions, as in McCarthy et al. (2016). This will help identify lemmas for which classification is trickier.

Acknowledgments

We would like to thank the anonymous reviewers for their helpful feedback. This work has been supported by the French National Research Agency under project ANR-16-CE33-0013.

References

Sanjeev Arora, Yingyu Liang, and Tengyu Ma. 2017. A Simple but Tough-to-Beat Baseline for Sentence Embeddings. In *International Conference on Learning Representations (ICLR)*, Toulon, France.

Marco Baroni, Silvia Bernardini, Adriano Ferraresi, and Eros Zanchetta. 2009. The WaCky wide web: a collection of very large linguistically processed web-crawled corpora. *Journal of Language Resources and Evaluation*, 43(3):209–226.

Daniel Cer, Yinfei Yang, Sheng-yi Kong, Nan Hua, Nicole Limtiaco, Rhomni St. John, Noah Constant, Mario Guajardo-Cespedes, Steve Yuan, Chris Tar, Brian Strope, and Ray Kurzweil. 2018. Universal Sentence Encoder for English. In *Proceedings of the 2018 Conference on Empirical Methods in Natural Language Processing: System Demonstrations*, pages 169–174, Brussels, Belgium. Association for Computational Linguistics.

Jacob Devlin, Ming-Wei Chang, Kenton Lee, and Kristina Toutanova. 2018. BERT: Pre-training of Deep Bidirectional Transformers for Language Understanding. *arXiv preprint arXiv:1810.04805*.

Katrin Erk, Diana McCarthy, and Nicholas Gaylord. 2009. Investigations on word senses and word usages. In *Proceedings of the Joint Conference of the 47th Annual Meeting of the ACL and the 4th International Joint Conference on Natural Language Processing of the AFNLP*, pages 10–18, Suntec, Singapore. Association for Computational Linguistics.

Christiane Fellbaum, editor. 1998. *WordNet: An Electronic Lexical Database*. Language, Speech, and Communication. MIT Press, Cambridge, MA.

Juri Ganitkevitch, Benjamin Van Durme, and Chris Callison-Burch. 2013. PPDB: The Paraphrase Database. In *Proceedings of the 2013 Conference of the North American Chapter of the Association for Computational Linguistics: Human Language Technologies*, pages 758–764, Atlanta, Georgia. Association for Computational Linguistics.

Aina Garí Soler, Marianna Apidianaki, and Alexandre Allauzen. 2019. Word usage similarity estimation with sentence representations and automatic substitutes. In *Proceedings of the Eighth Joint Conference on Lexical and Computational Semantics, Minneapolis, MN*. Association for Computational Linguistics.

Nancy Ide, Collin Baker, Christiane Fellbaum, Charles Fillmore, and Rebecca Passonneau. 2008. MASC: the Manually Annotated Sub-Corpus of American English. In *Proceedings of the Sixth International Conference on Language Resources and Evaluation (LREC'08)*, Marrakech, Morocco. European Language Resources Association (ELRA).

Kazuaki Kishida. 2005. *Property of average precision and its generalization: An examination of evaluation indicator for information retrieval experiments*. Technical Report NII-2005-014E, National Institute of Informatics Tokyo, Japan.

Gerhard Kremer, Katrin Erk, Sebastian Padó, and Stefan Thater. 2014. What substitutes tell us - analysis of an "all-words" lexical substitution corpus. In *Proceedings of the 14th Conference of the European Chapter of the Association for Computational Linguistics*, pages 540–549, Gothenburg, Sweden. Association for Computational Linguistics.

Diana McCarthy, Marianna Apidianaki, and Katrin Erk. 2016. Word sense clustering and clusterability. *Computational Linguistics*, 42(2):245–275.

Oren Melamud, Jacob Goldberger, and Ido Dagan. 2016. context2vec: Learning Generic Context Embedding with Bidirectional LSTM. In *Proceedings of the 20th SIGNLL Conference on Computational Natural Language Learning*, pages 51–61, Berlin, Germany. Association for Computational Linguistics.

Oren Melamud, Omer Levy, and Ido Dagan. 2015. A Simple Word Embedding Model for Lexical Substitution. In *Proceedings of the 1st Workshop on Vector Space Modeling for Natural Language Processing*, pages 1–7, Denver, Colorado.

Tomas Mikolov, Kai Chen, Greg Corrado, and Jeffrey Dean. 2013. Efficient estimation of word representations in vector space. In *Proceedings of the International Conference on Learning Representations*, Scottsdale, Arizona.

Ellie Pavlick, Pushpendre Rastogi, Juri Ganitkevitch, Benjamin Van Durme, and Chris Callison-Burch. 2015. PPDB 2.0: Better paraphrase ranking, fine-grained entailment relations, word embeddings, and style classification . In *Proceedings of the 53rd Annual Meeting of the Association for Computational Linguistics and the 7th International Joint Conference on Natural Language Processing (Volume 2: Short Papers)*, pages 425–430, Beijing, China. Association for Computational Linguistics.

Jeffrey Pennington, Richard Socher, and Christopher Manning. 2014. Glove: Global vectors for word representation. In *Proceedings of the 2014 Conference on Empirical Methods in Natural Language Processing (EMNLP)*, pages 1532–1543, Doha, Qatar. Association for Computational Linguistics.

Matthew Peters, Mark Neumann, Mohit Iyyer, Matt Gardner, Christopher Clark, Kenton Lee, and Luke Zettlemoyer. 2018. Deep contextualized word representations. In *Proceedings of the 2018 Conference of the North American Chapter of the Association for Computational Linguistics: Human Language Technologies, Volume 1 (Long Papers)*, pages 2227–2237, New Orleans, Louisiana. Association for Computational Linguistics.

Mohammad Taher Pilehvar and Jose Camacho-Collados. 2019. WiC: the Word-in-Context Dataset for Evaluating Context-Sensitive Meaning Representations. In *Proceedings of NAACL*, Minneapolis, United States.

Karin Kipper Schuler. 2006. *VerbNet: A Broad-Coverage, Comprehensive Verb Lexicon*. Ph.D. thesis, University of Pennsylvania.

An ELMo-inspired approach to SemDeep-5's Word-in-Context task

Alan Ansell
Department of Computer Science
University of Waikato, New Zealand

Felipe Bravo-Marquez
Department of Computer Science
University of Chile & IMFD

Bernhard Pfahringer
Department of Computer Science
University of Waikato, New Zealand

Abstract

This paper describes a submission to the Word-in-Context competition for the IJCAI 2019 SemDeep-5 workshop. The task is to determine whether a given focus word is used in the same or different senses in two contexts. We took an ELMo-inspired approach similar to the baseline model in the task description paper, where contextualized representations are obtained for the focus words and a classification is made according to the degree of similarity between these representations. Our model had a few simple differences, notably joint training of the forward and backward LSTMs, a different choice of states for the contextualized representations and a new similarity measure for them. These changes yielded a 3.5% improvement on the ELMo baseline.

1 Introduction

Traditional word embedding systems such as word2vec (Mikolov et al., 2013) assign each word a single fixed embedding. One weakness of these systems is that they are not well suited for representing words which have multiple meanings, as their embeddings are forced to occupy a point in the vector space which corresponds to some combination of these meanings. Much attention has been given to developing systems which can assign a word an embedding specific to the sense in which it is used in a given context (Huang et al., 2012; Neelakantan et al., 2014; Chen et al., 2014; Iacobacci et al., 2015; Li and Jurafsky, 2015; Peters et al., 2018, among others). Such a system could be thought of as yielding "sense embeddings" rather than word embeddings. Some sense embedding systems have shown advantages over traditional word embeddings, performing better on contextual word similarity tasks (Neelakantan et al., 2014; Chen et al., 2014, etc.) and relational similarity tasks (Iacobacci et al., 2015). One of the greatest successes has been the ELMo system (Peters et al., 2018) whose contextual embeddings were used to obtain state-of-the-art results on six NLP tasks.

The Word-in-Context (WiC) dataset (Pilehvar and Camacho-Collados, 2019) provides an opportunity to evaluate sense embedding systems by testing their ability to discriminate between finely-grained meanings of a word. Each instance in the dataset consists of two sentences which both contain a certain "focus" word. The instances must be classified according to whether the focus word is used in the same sense in the two sentences or not.

There are two main approaches to producing sense-specific embeddings. The first is to learn a number of embeddings for each word which correspond to its discrete senses, known as multi-prototype embeddings (Huang et al., 2012; Neelakantan et al., 2014; Chen et al., 2014; Iacobacci et al., 2015; Li and Jurafsky, 2015). The second is to dynamically create a unique embedding for a word for every context it appears in, which attempts to capture the particular shade of meaning the word has in that context. Notable examples of these "contextualized word embedding" systems include context2vec (Melamud et al., 2016) and ELMo (Peters et al., 2018).

The ELMo_1 baseline system in the task description paper (Pilehvar and Camacho-Collados, 2019) and our system can both be thought of as having three components: the LSTM-based (Hochreiter and Schmidhuber, 1997) language model; the "contextualization" component, in which contextualized embeddings for the focus words are obtained using the language model; and the "classification" component, where some similarity measure between the two contextualized embeddings is calculated and a positive classification is made if it is above a threshold learned on the training set.

In ELMo$_1$, the language model is as described in (Peters et al., 2018), the contextualized embeddings are the hidden states of the first LSTM layer at the focus word's position, and the similarity measure is cosine similarity. In sections 2.1, 2.2 and 2.3, we will describe how these three components operate in our system.

2 System Description

2.1 Language Model

The system uses a bidirectional LSTM-based language model. Instead of predicting the next or previous word given a left or right side context, the model predicts a missing word given both a left and right context - in this sense it is similar to context2vec. During training, two LSTM layers are run over a complete input sentence in both directions. The forward and backward directions are independent until the output layer, when they are used jointly as inputs to the softmax layer. Specifically the outputs of the second of two LSTM layers over a sentence of n words give a sequence of forward representations $\overrightarrow{\boldsymbol{u}}_1, \overrightarrow{\boldsymbol{u}}_2, ..., \overrightarrow{\boldsymbol{u}}_n \in \mathbb{R}^d$ and a sequence of backward representations $\overleftarrow{\boldsymbol{u}}_1, \overleftarrow{\boldsymbol{u}}_2, ..., \overleftarrow{\boldsymbol{u}}_n \in \mathbb{R}^d$. For each non-edge position $2 \leq i \leq n-1$ in the sentence, we define a vector $\boldsymbol{x}_i$ as $[\overrightarrow{\boldsymbol{u}}_{i-1} \overleftarrow{\boldsymbol{u}}_{i+1}]$, the concatenation of the forward representation in the preceding position and the backward representation in the following position. $\boldsymbol{x}_i$ is fed into a softmax layer over the vocabulary:

$$\boldsymbol{p}^{(i)} = \mathrm{softmax}(W\boldsymbol{x}_i)$$

The objective is to maximise the predicted probability of the observed sentences, or equivalently minimise the cross entropy loss J:

$$J = -\sum_{i=2}^{n-1} \log p_{s_i}^{(i)},$$

where s_i is the index in the vocabulary of the word which appears in position i in the sentence.

2.2 Contextualization

Let f_1 and f_2 be the position of the focus word in sentences 1 and 2 of an example in the WiC dataset. Rather than using $\overrightarrow{\boldsymbol{u}}_f$ or $\overleftarrow{\boldsymbol{u}}_f$ as contextualized word representations for the focus word f, we instead use $\boldsymbol{x}_f$, the vector which would be used to predict the focus word. $\boldsymbol{x}_f$ is a representation of the expectations we have about the focus word given the context, and so we would expect $\boldsymbol{x}_{f_1}^{(1)}$ and $\boldsymbol{x}_{f_2}^{(2)}$ to differ significantly when the focus word is being used in a different sense.

2.3 Classification

We tried several similarity measures between $\boldsymbol{x}_{f_1}^{(1)}$ and $\boldsymbol{x}_{f_2}^{(2)}$, including dot product and cosine distance. The best-performing measure in our experiments was a weighted dot product

$$d(\boldsymbol{x}_{f_1}^{(1)}, \boldsymbol{x}_{f_2}^{(2)}) = \boldsymbol{w}^\top(\boldsymbol{x}_{f_1}^{(1)} \circ \boldsymbol{x}_{f_2}^{(2)})$$

where $\circ$ denotes element-wise product and $\boldsymbol{w}$ is a trainable weight vector. Learning $\boldsymbol{w}$ was treated as a logistic regression problem on the training set with feature vector $\boldsymbol{x}_{f_1}^{(1)} \circ \boldsymbol{x}_{f_2}^{(2)}$.

2.4 Corpus, Preprocessing and Hyperparameters

The model was trained on a 2018 Wikipedia dump. All tokens were lowercased. Those which appeared at least 300 times were included in the vocabulary, and others were replaced with <UNK>, resulting in a vocabulary size of ~100,000. The corpus was split into training examples at sentence boundaries, each example containing as many sentences as possible followed by padding to reach a 50 token limit. Each example was capped with a <START> and <END> token. The examples were randomly shuffled so that each batch would contain a diverse range of texts.

Each token in the vocabulary and <START>, <END> and <UNK> were assigned a randomly initialized 256-dimensional embedding. The LSTM cells had 2048 hidden units which were projected to a 256-dimensional output. There was no sharing of weights for the LSTM cells between layers or the two directions. There was an additional residual connection which fed the raw embeddings directly into the second LSTM layer.

The weight vector $\boldsymbol{w}$ had dimension 512 (as $\boldsymbol{x}$ is the concatenation of two LSTM output vectors), and the training set contained ~5,500 examples. $\boldsymbol{w}$ was fitted using Scikit-Learn's LogisticRegression with L2 regularization with parameter C ("inverse of regularization strength") set to 0.2. This value was obtained through tuning on the development set.

3 Results and Analysis

3.1 Results

A single submission was made to the competition during the evaluation period with parameters as described above, scoring 61.2% on the test set. This result and the results of a number of other system configurations are shown in Table 1.

Another submission made in the post-evaluation period attempted to improve on the original submission by using a model trained on a corpus consisting of the Wikipedia dump combined with a corpus of books, "BookCorpus" (Zhu et al., 2015). It also used stronger regularization when learning $\boldsymbol{w}$, setting $C = 0.02$. This submission scored 62.4%.

3.2 Analysis

Our system demonstrated significant improvement on the baseline models using relatively simple techniques. There are only a few significant differences between our system and the baseline model ELMo_1:

- Input is whole-token based rather than character based.
- Different training corpora - the ELMo version used was trained on the 1 Billion Word Benchmark.
- Forward and backward LSTMs are trained jointly.
- Contextualized embedding for a word is the vector used to predict the word rather than the output vector for the word's position in the sentence.
- Different similarity measure for contextualized embeddings.

We note that when ELMo_1's contextualization and classification methods (i.e. first layer hidden states, cosine similarity) are used with our trained language model, the test set accuracy is 54.9% compared with the 57.7% quoted in (Pilehvar and Camacho-Collados, 2019) for ELMo_1. This suggests that our system may have performed better with better language model implementation or training.

Comparing the "predictor" to the "hidden" states with cosine similarity, we see that this different choice of contextualized embedding is worth 4.2% on the test set.

While the use of weighted dot product was worth 7.2% compared to unweighted dot product on the dev set, this translated to only a 2.1% improvement on the test set, suggesting that some overfitting occurred when learning the dot product weights $\boldsymbol{w}$ despite the use of a regularization parameter fitted on the dev set. This may be because there is a greater degree of similarity between the train and dev sets than the train and test sets, as suggested in (Pilehvar and Camacho-Collados, 2019).

3.3 Limitations

There are a number of potential areas for improvements in our system:

- Since $\boldsymbol{x}_f$ is determined only by the context of the focus word, the focus word itself has no impact on the model's predictions. It seems as though it should be possible to improve performance by utilising knowledge about the focus word, but we did not manage to find a convincing method.
- The dataset contains many examples where the focus words in the two sentences share the same root but have different inflectional morphology, e.g. "break" and "breaks". This may cause some false negative classifications because the focus words having different tense or plurality is likely to result in differences in their $\boldsymbol{x}$ vectors in the dimensions relating to these features. Using the weighted dot product may alleviate this problem somewhat because it allows reduced weight to be assigned to dimensions which correspond to tense and plurality. A better solution however might be to preprocess the training corpus and all examples in the dataset to remove inflection entirely.

States	Similarity measure	Dev.	Test	Notes
Predictor	Weighted dot product	67.4	61.2	Submitted to competition
Predictor	Unweighted dot product	60.2	59.1	
Predictor	Cosine similarity	60.5	59.1	
Hidden	Cosine similarity	55.2	54.9	cf. ELMo_1 "threshold" version.
Hidden	Weighted dot product	54.1	53.1	

Table 1: Results with different system configurations. All results listed were obtained with the same training run of the language model trained on Wikipedia 2018. "Predictor" refers to the use of the $\boldsymbol{x}$ vectors used for predicting missing words, while "hidden" refers to the outputs of the first LSTM layer for both directions concatenated.

4 Conclusions and Future Work

We discovered several improved ways of using ELMo-type contextualized word embeddings to perform word sense disambiguation in the Word-in-Context task. When the forward and backward LSTMs were trained jointly, we found that it is better to use the concatenation of output states from the forward LSTM at the position before the focus and the backward LSTM at the position after the focus than it is to use hidden states from the focus position. We also found that a weighted dot product performs better than unweighted dot product or cosine similarity as a metric for determining whether two contextualized word embeddings refer to the same sense of the word or not. This suggests that some dimensions of such embeddings carry more information related to the human notion of word sense than others. Together these improvements yielded a 3.5% gain over the ELMo_1 baseline of (Pilehvar and Camacho-Collados, 2019), and there is reason to think that a better implemented language model could do even better.

A surprising aspect of our system is that it never looks at the focus word itself, only the context. Future work on this system might center on exploiting what we know about the focus word to improve performance.

5 Acknowledgements

Felipe Bravo-Marquez was funded by Millennium Institute for Foundational Research on Data.

References

Xinxiong Chen, Zhiyuan Liu, and Maosong Sun. 2014. A unified model for word sense representation and disambiguation. In *Proceedings of the 2014 Conference on Empirical Methods in Natural Language Processing (EMNLP)*, pages 1025–1035, Doha, Qatar. Association for Computational Linguistics.

Sepp Hochreiter and Jürgen Schmidhuber. 1997. Long short-term memory. *Neural Comput.*, 9(8):1735–1780.

Eric H. Huang, Richard Socher, Christopher D. Manning, and Andrew Y. Ng. 2012. Improving word representations via global context and multiple word prototypes. In *Proceedings of the 50th Annual Meeting of the Association for Computational Linguistics: Long Papers - Volume 1*, ACL '12, pages 873–882, Stroudsburg, PA, USA. Association for Computational Linguistics.

Ignacio Iacobacci, Mohammad Taher Pilehvar, and Roberto Navigli. 2015. SensEmbed: Learning sense embeddings for word and relational similarity. In *Proceedings of the 53rd Annual Meeting of the Association for Computational Linguistics and the 7th International Joint Conference on Natural Language Processing (Volume 1: Long Papers)*, pages 95–105, Beijing, China. Association for Computational Linguistics.

Jiwei Li and Dan Jurafsky. 2015. Do multi-sense embeddings improve natural language understanding? In *Proceedings of the 2015 Conference on Empirical Methods in Natural Language Processing*, pages 1722–1732, Lisbon, Portugal. Association for Computational Linguistics.

Oren Melamud, Jacob Goldberger, and Ido Dagan. 2016. context2vec: Learning generic context embedding with bidirectional lstm. In *Proceedings of The 20th SIGNLL Conference on Computational Natural Language Learning*, pages 51–61.

Tomas Mikolov, Kai Chen, Greg Corrado, and Jeffrey Dean. 2013. Efficient estimation of word representations in vector space.

Arvind Neelakantan, Jeevan Shankar, Alexandre Passos, and Andrew McCallum. 2014. Efficient non-parametric estimation of multiple embeddings per word in vector space. In *Proceedings of the 2014 Conference on Empirical Methods in Natural Language Processing (EMNLP)*, pages 1059–1069, Doha, Qatar. Association for Computational Linguistics.

Matthew Peters, Mark Neumann, Mohit Iyyer, Matt Gardner, Christopher Clark, Kenton Lee, and Luke Zettlemoyer. 2018. Deep contextualized word representations. In *Proceedings of NAACL*, pages 2227–2237, New Orleans, Louisiana. Association for Computational Linguistics.

Mohammad Taher Pilehvar and Jose Camacho-Collados. 2019. Wic: the word-in-context dataset for evaluating context-sensitive meaning representations. In *Proceedings of NAACL*, Minneapolis, United States.

Yukun Zhu, Ryan Kiros, Richard Zemel, Ruslan Salakhutdinov, Raquel Urtasun, Antonio Torralba, and Sanja Fidler. 2015. Aligning books and movies: Towards story-like visual explanations by watching movies and reading books.

Association for Computational Linguistics
209 N. Eighth Street
Stroudsburg, Pennsylvania 18360

ISBN 978-1-5108-9142-5

9 781510 891425

CURRAN ASSOCIATES INC.
proceedings.com